Praise for
CONNECTING WITH GOD IN THE GARDEN

"Cecile Smith's deep and vibrant spirituality shines through her reflections and meditations found in *Connecting with God in the Garden*. The garden is where the seeds of faith are planted, grow, and blossom with each passing season, and Cecile's vibrant writing will lift hearts and minds closer to God."   Douglas Bean, Editor, *The Catholic Times* Newspaper

"Tradition holds that God has revealed Himself to man in two ways: through the Book of the Word, and through the Book of Nature. Lectio Divina is an ancient practice in the Church, whereby the faithful are able to enter into a loving encounter with our living God, by a prayerful reading of Holy Scriptures. In *Connecting with God in the Garden,* her first book, Cecile Smith helps her readers apply the principles of Lectio Divina to the Book of Nature, enabling them to learn lessons through a greater awareness of the grandeur of God's presence in the natural world. She teaches us to open our senses to the wonders of creation, and elevate our hearts in adoration of its Creator."
   Julie Foley, Homeschool Mom, Educator, Biology and Theology

"Way to GROW! Whether an avid gardener or one who only likes to stop and smell the roses, Smith's *Connecting with God in the Garden* adds valuable insight to the bouquet of life. Each passage offers a divine gift as unique as the tree, shrub, or flower it celebrates. As a former homeschool mother, I see the value of using this book to nourish children's appreciation and botanical awareness of God's presence in His garden. As a spiritual healer, I will use this book as an instructive and beautifully symbolic tool to help guide and heal clients. A book that will stand the test of time!"
   Lisa Tremont Ota, RD, MPH, MA, Author, Sacred Exploration Radio

"It is rare in this day and time to find a book that not only inspires and enlightens, but also provides its readers the opportunity to share the writer's deeply personal quest — and ultimate success!"   Kathy W. Larkin, Writer, Editor

"When you need a break from this fast-paced world, find a garden. When you want to reconnect with God through prayer, step into that garden. And when you seek guidance to enrich your stay, read Cecile Smith's book. Here you will discover inspiring spiritual reflections, each one written with care and love. Carry this book with you, since you never know when you will come upon a tranquil garden in which to pray. Your garden may end up being real or imaginary, but with this guidebook, you will experience peace, stillness, and calm."
   Dr. Beth Milwid, Stress Management Consultant, www.doctorbeth.com

This book defines the priceless reality of "intimacy" with God in a thousand ways.

Mike Williamson, PhD

"What provocative thought! I have read many reflection books in my day but Cecile has a most interesting perspective on the sacred. It makes me want to wake up to what is in front of me. She is a vessel of God pouring out His message. Thank you for the inspiration."

Patricia Henderson, MSW

"Very nice! Very relatable — nothing too lofty or unachievable. These reflections portray experiences we all have and can have if we are still and receive our surroundings."

Lucian Smith, Poet, Musician, Author of "My Cosmos"

What Readers Are Saying

"Cecile's book takes you into a world of repose with God for a few moments of your day!"

Chris Higgins, Ohio

"This book helped me develop a new uncharted path of connecting nature to prayer, thus strengthening my spiritual journey in life. I feel a sense of inner peace and calmness, allowing me to develop a more intimate relationship with the Divine. It has brought more meaning to my life and a more prayerful existence through nature."   Denise Harris, Ohio

"This is marvelous — just what I have been needing. Cecile's writing is so clear and inspiring. I love her specific directions about how to listen to God. Very helpful. I need to read those words every day."   Pat H., Ohio

"Cecile's thoughts, words, and images allow me to identify and appreciate the feelings of redemption I enjoy when I am alone and at peace, working in my garden. Her beautiful soul is shared through her collection of meditations, scriptures, songs, and poems."

Ginya Carnahan, Florida

"Cecile is truly my mouthpiece. Her reflections reorient my thinking. I believe many people will benefit from her insight."   Colette Massey, Ohio

"This book is a work of art that transports you to nature, invoking feelings of calm and peace through prayer and reflections. After reading *Connecting with God in the Garden,* I feel that communicating through prayer in nature is the answer I have been looking for to grow in my relationship with God. Cecile's beautiful reflections focus on nature and God's Word, helping one to trust the communication received in moments of stillness, as the guideposts to growing a greater connection with Him."   Maura Lein, Ohio

"Your book is so beautiful. The bits you sent make me feel peaceful and reflective. Thank you very much for sharing it with us." Kogie Moodley, South Africa

"This book is unlike any other Catholic devotional I have ever seen. Instead of inspiring ideas, it takes you straight to the heart of God so you can hear from Him for yourself. This book is for anyone who desires a more intimate relationship with the Lord." Amy Hayes, Texas

"As someone who wants to take religion at my own pace, this is an excellent guide to explore my relationship with God. The prompts are thought-provoking and timeless. This is a book I will use for years to come as my perspective changes. I wish I had had this book while I was rebuilding my relationship with God after losing my father. It has allowed me to put aside my anger and see the beauty in the cycle of life again." Sarah Beth Imperi, Tennessee

"Just what I need to help me through my grief." Diane Fetty, North Carolina

"As a wife, mother of eight, hobby farmer, photographer, and naturalist, I am a busy woman. What I love about Cecile's book is that it offers a short daily reflection, which I can take with me and apply in my own way to my own life. In a single word, for a busy woman, it is doable." Leslie Smith, Ohio

"I felt I was sitting in the garden myself and these were my observations." Diane McCullough, Pennsylvania

"These are beautifully uplifting in content, layout, and power. I love the way you merge the quote, poem, and reflection into each piece. This is beautiful and thought-provoking. Susan J. Weaver, EdD

Connecting with God in the Garden

Connecting with God in the Garden

An Inspirational Journal for All Seasons

Cecile Smith

Montorio Società
Columbus, Ohio

Connecting with God in the Garden: An Inspirational Journal for All Seasons

© 2022 Cecile Smith

All rights reserved. With the exception of short excerpts used in articles and critical reviews, no part of this work may be reproduced, transmitted, or stored in any form whatsoever, printed or electronic, without the prior written permission of the author and publisher.

Montorio Società
MontorioSocieta@yahoo.com

Unless otherwise noted, scripture texts in this work are taken from the *New American Bible, revised edition* © 2010, 1991, 1986, 1970 Confraternity of Christian Doctrine, Washington, D.C. and are used by permission of the copyright owner. All Rights Reserved. No part of the New American Bible may be reproduced in any form without permission in writing from the copyright owner. Permission to use The New American Bible does not imply review or approval of the work.

Excerpts from the Jerusalem Bible ©1966 by Darton Longman & Todd Ltd and Doubleday and Company Ltd. Reprinted by permission of the publisher.

Every reasonable effort has been made to determine copyright holders of excerpted materials and to secure permissions as needed. If any copyrighted materials have been inadvertently used in this work without proper credit being given in one form or another, please notify MontorioSocieta@yahoo.com. in writing so that future printings of this work may be corrected accordingly.

For wholesale inquiries contact: MontorioSocieta@yahoo.com.

ISBN: 979-8-9857927-0-6 (paperback)

ISBN: 979-8-9857927-1-3 (ebook)

Editors: Michelle Buckman, Kathy W. Larkin, Virginia Carnahan, Rachel Shuster

Back cover photo credit: Leslie Smith, Narratives Photography

Cover and interior design by Christy Day, Constellation Book Services

Design consultants: Kathy W. Larkin and Suzanne Smith

Illustrations throughout by istock.com and dreamstime.com

Published in the United States of America

To all of you who have ever
desired divine intimacy
searched for a close connection with your Creator
longed for an earthly friendship with Jesus
hoped for a loving companionship with Mary
but did not know where to look.

Special thanks to
My readers. My friends. My family.
All of you.
Each of you.
You are the beauty that
God has sent into my life.
You are my Garden of gardens.
You soothe my soul
And I love you very much.

Dear Reader,

In these pages
you will learn

- to connect with God in Nature
- to be still and hear His voice
- to find daily inspiration and
- a deep and powerful spirituality

My hope is that
you will build a tangible relationship with God
through effortless prayer.

Join me in the garden where we will hear God's voice
while soaking up the beauty,
the wisdom,
and love of creation!

Contents

Foreword .... *xvi*
God's Nature .... *xix*
Introduction *1*
    How I First Heard God in My Garden *1*
    How I Conduct My Conversations with God *3*
    What Led Me to the Garden *4*
    How this Book Connects You with God through the Seasons *6*

PART I: YOUR JOURNEY AND CONVERSATION
    CHAPTER I: JOURNEY TO GOD THROUGH NATURE 11
        Most People Think They Know How to Pray 11
        Find *Your* Garden Place 12
        Pray with Ease 13
        How to Begin Hearing God Speak to You 14
        How You Will Know it Is God Who Speaks 15

    CHAPTER II: THE PURPOSE AND IMPORTANCE OF CONVERSING WITH GOD 17
        The Purpose of Conversing with God Is to 17
            Know Him and Become His Friend
        Knowing What God Wants of You 18
        It's about Time 19
        Inspirational Organization to Help You along Your Journey 20

PART II: YOUR DIVINE CONNECTION
        Four Seasons of Inspiration
        Quotes and Scripture Verses
        Reflective Poems
        Gentle Prayer Guide
        Journal

    YOUR JOURNEY BEGINS 27
    SPRING RENEWAL: Growing in the Spirit in God's Garden 28
        What Brings Me to This Place? 30
        The Heavenly Haven 32
        God's Calling 34
        Cold Hard Comfort 36

    "Live Forever" 38
    Community 40
    Saint Patrick's Day 43
    Undoer of Knots 46
    Rejuvenating Rain 48
    Perfect Serenity 50
    Lifting for Love 52
    Birds of Peace 54
    Divine Design 56
    Weeds 58
    Silent Beauty 60
    Hidden Azalea 62
    Dew Point 64
    Magnificent Maple 66
    Thoughts On a Day in May (by Anne A. Imperi) 68

JOURNEY INTO SUMMER 71
SUMMER EASE: Praying Effortlessly in God's Garden 72
    Summer Vacation 74
    Miniature Rose 76
    Peaceful Sunday 78
    Yesterday and Today 80
    Gracefulness in Order 83
    Fig Leaves in the Rain 86
    Garden Prayers 88
    Our Garden 90
    God's Fingerprints 92
    Giving and Receiving 94
    Sunday Morning 96
    Duty and Shadows 98
    The Color of God 100
    Rose of Sharon 102
    A Butterfly's Love 104
    God's Touch 106
    Dandelions 108
    The Real Thing 110

CONTINUE YOUR JOURNEY 113
AUTUMN HOPE: Enjoying Colors in God's Garden 114
    Autumn Hope 116
    September Lessons 118

Cedars of Lebanon 121
Raspberry Rose 124
Silent Companion 126
The Sparrow's Prayer 128
Spiritual Blankets 130
Gratitude 132
Autumn Spectacular 135
Shining Through 138
Perspective 140
Eternal Life 142
Why the Sky 144
New Awakenings 146
Chrysanthemums and Pumpkins 148
Wonderful Faults 150
November Sky 152

JOURNEY THROUGH TRANSITION 155
WINTER WONDER: Staying Connected in God's Garden 156
    Transitions 158
    'Twas a Month Before Christmas 160
    Winter's Wonders 162
    Madonna 164
    The Canticle of Mary 164
    The Nativity 166
    Joy to the World 168
    Sunrise, Sunset 170
    Sunshine and My New Front Door 172
    Living Water 174
    Winter's Trees 176
    Hidden Presence 178
    Here in the Gray 180
    The Shape of God 182
    What Do You Seek? 184
    The Virtue of Preparation 186
    Blessings 188
    Coffee & Creation 190

Afterword — The Eternal Moment *192*
End Note *193*
Gratitude and Appreciation *194*
Quotes and Resources *197*

Foreword

As I grow older, I find myself looking back to childhood, and to those who played important roles in forming my young life. Over the years, I've been fortunate to have kept in touch — albeit sporadically — with one of my closest grade-school friends, Cecile, author of this publication, *Connecting with God in the Garden*.

Together, we have faithfully preserved our half-century-long friendship; in part because we are of the same mind on many topics and have always enjoyed passionate conversation. In fact, when we were ten years old, we would sometimes walk together to the nearest street corner at the end of the school day. There, we enjoyed interesting and animated conversation before our walk home took us in opposite directions.

We were nothing alike. Open, confident, and out-going, Cecile was one of ten children in a Catholic family. I, on the other hand, was shy, reserved, and tentative, having come from a family of four, who converted when I was five. Yet, Cecile and I could talk nonstop about nothing — and everything. And on those days, I remember enjoying a lighter mood on the walk home: hopeful and content; thankful for such a friend!

Today, Cecile is the same bright, talented, and goal-oriented person she has always been. So, when she mentioned needing copy editing assistance with her book-in-progress, I was excited and intrigued. As I began reading her words, I found I could relate to what she has experienced in her garden. When troubled or worried, my mind always clears more readily when outside, no matter the weather. Breezes are calming, the sound of nearby birds chirping is comforting, the fresh scent of grass uplifting — much like the feeling evoked after a conversation with a supportive friend.

This *Inspirational Journal for All Seasons* is the result of Cecile's intimate, spiritual journey, which blossomed from a humble backyard respite into a deeper, more intimate and tangible relationship with God. Spanning the past dozen years, her graceful, nature-inspired reflections encompass the four seasons. Finding beauty in creation even in winter, Cecile's contemplative words draw the reader into a deeper understanding of nature and how it relates to God's lessons for us all.

Foreword

Penned primarily within her tranquil garden space, Cecile's writing is rhythmic and thoughtful. Throughout the pages, she recounts the many God-inspired insights she received while tending her garden, or sitting quietly and observing a thriving nature. Each personal reflection is accompanied by a relevant quotation, as well as meditative prompts that invite readers to delve deeper into their own intimate relationship with God. Journal lines throughout provide ready space to begin recording thoughts and feelings the words evoke.

At times simplistic, often profound, the message within these pages is stated loud and clear: God is here as our Creator and friend; waiting to listen, be heard, and build an earthly friendship with each of us. All we need do is open our heart, converse with Nature, and we will experience His comforting companionship.

Kathy W. Larkin, B.A.
Writer/Editor
Lexington Herald-Leader Central Kentucky Lifestyle and
Bluegrass Balance magazines; *The Lane Report*, *Ace Magazine,* and *Odyssey Magazine.*

GOD'S NATURE

Nature has no choices.
Nature is always obedient to the Creator's plan.
When one flower thrives and another shrivels and dies,
they are each in perfect harmony with God's Will
and each other.
When we pray in the midst of this kind of "devotion,"
our hearts can be enlightened by the virtues in motion
here, in our gardens.

Understanding touches our hearts
and we can recognize
the path we must cultivate.
So, enter your garden
and open your heart to
the wisdom there:
God's Nature

INTRODUCTION

I wondered if He had a special message for me.
So, I asked, "God, what are you trying to tell me?"

Have you ever heard God's voice in the silence of your heart?
Wished to know what He would like you to do today?
Talked with Him as a friend?
Asked His advice?

How I First Heard God in My Garden
Immediately, I Heard His Voice!

My experience began a decade ago on an incredible summer afternoon, as I sat in the midst of my garden, surrounded by lovely flowers — where butterflies and bees enjoyed themselves even more than I. Suddenly, I was moved by the grandeur of it all. I had mused in this very place many times, but on that day, something stirred inside me. My soul was lost in reverie, and filled with amazement at the splendor.

My heart overflowed with calm awe, and my eyes were drawn to the beauty of the clear blue sky. Just gazing at it brought tranquility. Looking up, I took a deep breath and felt God's peace in my soul. With a second breath, the stress of life melted away and gratitude filled my heart. The moment was so sacred, I sensed there was more.

I wondered if He had a special message for me. So, I asked, "God, what are you trying to tell me?"

Instantly, I heard His voice speaking to me in the words of Jesus, "I am with you always" (Matthew 28:20). Then, I heard these words in my heart: *I am here with you every day, beneath My endless sky. I have given you all these things so that you can know Me. Nature is the revelation of My very self, and if you look closely enough and listen in the breeze, I will whisper to you and you will hear My voice.*

My heart filled with joy! He was here. In my garden. Speaking to me. In this eternal moment. I had finally discovered sacred silence in today's peaceful blue sky and the profound stillness for which my soul had longed. I felt the intimacy of God's presence in His mystery of Nature. I felt His love enfolding me and filling my entire being.

His whisper awakened my soul and I hurried inside for a notebook and pencil. I wrote only for myself, as I had no idea that others might also have spent a lifetime searching for a simple and effortless way to pray — a conversation with God, Himself: a two-way conversation, as with a friend.

I first heard Him speak to me here in my garden, but I am sure He had whispered in my heart many times before. I just hadn't listened. This time I asked Him a question — and He answered. I had never asked Him a question before — taken part in a conversation with Him — but He waited patiently, until I was ready, and my life has never been the same.

I returned the next day, and the next, to hear His voice and ask what He had planned for me — a lesson to learn, an insight to discover, a kindness to pass on, a blessing for myself, a virtue to live by.

I continued writing down my conversations with God the Creator, God the Son, and the Mother of God in my notebooks — my own peaceful prayer journal. I assumed others had already found divine intimacy — a friendship with God — based on their devout lives, but one day I began sheepishly sharing my insights with a few friends and, over time, my circle of readers grew. I discovered that God had not spoken only to *me* in my garden, but also to others longing to hear His voice, and He, theirs.

To this day, I revisit God in this place, my garden, to learn the wisdom of Nature from its very source, to discover all the truths hidden in creation, and to hear the voice of my God, my friend.

Introduction

How I Conduct My Conversations with God
I Speak to My Lord as a Friend

I love to think of nature as an unlimited broadcasting station, through which God speaks to us every hour, if we only tune in.

—George Washington Carver[1]

My conversations with God begin each time with my contemplation of some natural element that has caught my attention, and continue with my question, which is always the same: "What are you trying to tell me? What do You want me to learn from this, Lord?"

Like visual parables, He teaches me many things:

- A plump mother cardinal perching nearby teaches me attentiveness
- A coneflower developing through its stages demonstrates that delicacy is not weakness
- A variety of insects gathered on the sedum affirms the power of community
- Limbs gently swaying in the breeze suggest that I too can sway with the vicissitudes of life
- A bountiful dewfall reminds me of the abundance of God's refreshing grace
- The effect of rain seen in thirsty flower beds manifests the restorative power of God's Living Water

He teaches me through color, texture, sight, and sound all in harmony as Nature.

Jesus is truly tangible to me in Nature, and I can listen and speak to Him as both Lord and friend. And sometimes, in the midst of beautiful blossoms, bumblebees and sweet heavenly fragrances, I feel the splendor of Divine Presence and my heart leaps with deep emotion.

I choose to go out into my garden and enter God's world — the fruit of His Will — where His creation can soothe my soul, comfort my affliction, fill my cup, energize my being, and teach me His ways.

When I sit in my backyard, surrounded by His wonders of creation, I ask God what He wants me to see — and He always answers.

What Led Me to the Garden
Restful Calm and Nature's Delights

The Lord God then took the man and settled him in the garden of Eden, to cultivate and care for it.
–Genesis 2:15

In the beginning, I was led to my garden as a break from my indoor duties. When in need of recharging, I stepped out my back door and began to plant and prune, weed and wonder. I joked about it being my therapy, but I found these activities to be truly restoring.

I spent years creating my backyard garden, and when there was more time — the kids having grown up — I relaxed and enjoyed the peaceful calm while observing Nature's delights. Of course, there were still chores and affairs to be handled indoors, but I found it hard to leave this place of restfulness. This haven was so different from the rest of my life. A respite. A reward. A blessing. This space felt sacred, although I didn't think of God being present here. I had never been introduced to the idea of spirituality in Nature. I went to church to worship and receive God's graces. Little did I know, He was right in my own backyard.

I would sit — breathing fresh air; gazing upon pleasant plants, marveling at their loveliness; watching bugs and birds, squirrels and rabbits scurry about in their busyness. I felt the warm kiss of the sun or a wisp of breeze or the chill of cooler weather. The rest of my life was so full of *doing*, yet wrapped in my garden, I could just *be*.

Introduction

In this way, I had stumbled upon the necessary elements to connect with God through Nature:

1. **Silence.** The garden is a special place away from all distractions where we can sink into the sights and sounds of Nature and concentrate on Him. Saint Teresa of Calcutta urges us to find God's presence: "We need to find God, and He cannot be found in noise and restlessness. God is the friend of silence. See how nature — trees, flowers, grass — grows in silence; see the stars, the moon and the sun, how they move in silence..."[2]

2. **God's Presence.** Most of us do not have daily access to the Real Presence of Jesus in the Eucharist, so we must find other places to be in His presence, and Nature is one possibility. The revelation of God in Nature is so stirring and prevailing that Saint Paul urges awareness and praise for our Creator in Romans 1:20: "Ever since the creation of the world, His invisible attributes of eternal power and divinity have been able to be understood and perceived in what He has made."

3. **Stillness.** Stillness is akin to silence, but different. We must learn to still our heart, mind, and being — that churning inside involving lists, responsibilities, and schedules. To be still, we must free our consciousness of all these things. Then, let Nature distract, draw you in. Imagine, for a moment, a butterfly fluttering about you. Consider that God is enticing you to attentiveness. Follow its flight; notice its loveliness and grace. Remain still enough that it could alight upon you. *This* is the stillness necessary to hear God's voice.

4. **Question.** Now, in your own words, ask Him to speak to you and help you recognize His message.

How this Book Connects You with God through the Seasons
Nature Has a Divine Message for You Every Season

*Let us come alive to the splendor that is all around us,
and see the beauty in ordinary things.*

–Thomas Merton[3]

The poetic offerings in Part II of this book are inspired by Nature's splendor and the divine message therein. Each is accompanied by a scripture verse or meaningful quote to affirm its message, and encouragement to reflect and connect with your own inspiration.

Journal lines are provided to record your thoughts, observations, or questions. Finally, a "Seed of Grace" is offered to inspire contemplation. Commit to carrying this little Seed in your heart throughout the day.

To begin, enter *your* "garden" and pause. Take in your surroundings with a deep relaxing sigh. Still your mind and soften your heart. Read a reflection thoughtfully to savor the message you receive. Ask God what He is telling you, and what He wants you to know. Then *listen* — to your heart and God's voice. Follow inspiration to your own contemplation. Write your thoughts for future musings — whenever you need solace.

Take this calmness with you into your day, whether too busy or not busy enough. Let divine comfort be with you in all you do, and whenever you feel unsettled or frantic, revisit this connection you discovered.

Reread your own thoughts — these are revelations from God.

When you linger in Nature, you will hear Jesus whisper in your heart, and you will know what plans He has for you today. He will tell you — if you ask — through the beauty that envelops you. Then, contemplate your day, and you will be on your way to an exciting journey with the Son of God, "right in your own backyard."

And you may say, as Peter did, "Lord, it is good that we are here." (Matthew 17:4)

PART I

How to Journey to God through Nature

The Purpose and Importance of Conversing with God

CHAPTER I

Journey to God through Nature

Jesus Created Nature to Reveal Himself to Us

Meditating upon the beauty of the natural world can heal our mind, body, and spirit, as well as nurture within us the seeds of wisdom and truth. The beauty buried within every corner of the natural world has a lesson for us along the journey to becoming the souls God has destined us to be — holy and without blemish.

–Chris Hazell, "Nature and the Soul"[1]

Most People Think They Know How to Pray
God Is Closer than You Think

I thought I knew how to pray. I lived a life filled with devotions and, yet, I felt distant from God — that He was up there and I was down here. I knew He loved me, and I proclaimed that I loved Him, but I longed for closeness. When I finally discovered Him in Nature, He became truly tangible to me, and I could listen to Him and speak to Him as a friend — right here on Earth.

Many people travel to faraway places in search of: Castilian roses on a hillside in Guadalupe; healing waters at the grotto in Lourdes; a higher divinity on a mountain in Nepal. We take trips and make pilgrimages to holy shrines for a closer connection with God and Mary. These are great spiritual adventures, yet not accessible every day.

Nature can be found everywhere through simple connections:

Fresh air, the open sky, and birds, trees, and flowers along a city sidewalk can lift spirits as you experience God's gifts.

A hiking trail or walking path, mountaintop or meadow can provide adventurous refreshment for body and soul while you marvel at Nature's reverence.

The wonders of creation can encourage thoughtful observation from a favorite window looking out upon God's Earth, a nearby flower bed, or even a potted plant.

The chatter of birds, the ebb and flow of waves, the roar of the waterfall, and silence of the canyon can offer a glance into the magnificence of God's attributes as you listen to connect with Him.

Your own backyard, porch, balcony, or patio can present a view of God's creations while you pray in tranquility.

A local park or arboretum can offer opportunity for a pleasant stroll or ride as you take delight in the wonders of Nature.

Find *Your* Garden Place
God Awaits You within the Mystery of Creation

The tree that is beside the running water is fresher and gives more fruit.
—Saint Teresa of Avila[2]

You must discover the place and view in which you can meet God daily and make intimate contact with the living person of Jesus.

- ❀ Choose a bit of creation where you can listen and gain a sense of peace, which allows God to speak to your heart.

- Gaze upon the wonders of Nature, which reveal God's divine attributes: eternal power and wisdom, majesty and grandeur, nobility and richness, immensity and might, love and beauty.
- Encounter God in *your* garden place to open a tangible relationship with Him on Earth, so you can become friends.
- Discover the silence where you will be able to pray with ease from your heart.
- Contemplate Nature and you will receive inspiration from God, and know His plans for you.
- Surrounded by God's gifts in creation, quiet your mind and calm your heart so you will feel His love envelop you and hear His voice in the stillness.

We have strayed from the essence of God's presence here on this bountiful Earth. In our hurried way of life — with modern conveniences of conditioned air and easy transportation — we seem to have forgotten the signs of His love that remain in Nature.

Create a sacred space — in the shade or the morning sun; by the fireplace or on a voyage. And begin your journey today.

Pray with Ease
Jesus Yearns for Our Companionship

Prayer is putting oneself in the hands of God...
and listening to His voice in the depth of our hearts.
–Saint Teresa of Calcutta[3]

Prayer comes from the heart, where Jesus lives. Sometimes praying is hard but shouldn't be. Speaking to God doesn't require devout words or great forethought. Let your prayers pour out as a conversation with a dear friend, and then listen, enjoying your peaceful time with God as you would a serene sunset or a balmy breeze.

You know in your heart that every dazzled rising of the sun or newly blossomed flower is a blessing from God. Your heart tells you when you view a placid lake or flowing stream that they were created for you. Consider how these spectacular and tranquil gifts come to you without thinking or even asking. They permeate your senses with emotion. They fill your heart with joy. Sometimes, they take your breath away. This is God's Heart speaking to you.

Why not open your heart to His voice?

You need only

    to be still

        to be soft

            to ponder

                to ask

                    and then — to listen.

When you are still in the presence of God, you will feel utter peace. You will experience a sense of being one with Nature, one with God. You will be complete. This is how you can hear God.

How to Begin Hearing God Speak to You
Pause, Notice, Contemplate, and Listen

*There is something about getting our bodies out into the world,
in close contact with trees, bushes, flowers, squirrels, pigeons, and crows,
that can invigorate us and offer us new perspective on life.*
–Christine Valters Paintner, *EARTH, Our Original Monastery*[4]

I have heard God and His Blessed Mother while sitting in my garden, meandering in the field behind my house, and gazing out upon snow from the warmth of my home.

Earnestly, I would contemplate the natural wonder before me to gain a single insight into God's magnificent mystery of creation. My Lord would reveal to me a bit of advice regarding my relationship with Him and others. His message could be one of encouragement, affirmation, faith, or hope — a life lesson that I could put into action.

Look around you. Find a spot at home, in a park, along a dusty road, or perhaps even a good viewing point in the middle of town — a place that brings you peace and inspires you. A place where you can listen. As you sit in your garden spot, your place of inspiration, what is God saying to you today? What do you see in the colors and light? What do you hear in the shadows?

Stop your busy thoughts; begin to listen; open your heart to God's voice. He will send you a single insight into His magnificent mystery of creation!

>Pause, be still, and silent.
>Breathe, look at the sky and realize His immensity.
>Notice what attracts your attention.
>Contemplate for a few moments.
>Ask God for His message.
>Listen.
>Be patient with yourself. God is timeless.

How You Will Know it Is God Who Speaks
His Messages Are Always Full of Love

My sheep hear my voice; I know them, and they follow me.
—John 10:27

Have you ever listened but could not recognize God's voice? How will you know if it's Him?

You will know when God is speaking to you, because:

- His response is instantaneous! You may be taken by surprise.
- A word, thought, idea, or feeling — that is not your own — will immediately enter your mind or heart.
- At once, His reply makes sense and you understand.
- His message is always full of love.
- His advice is logical, complying with God's orderliness.
- He tells you how to fill your day with kindness and consideration for others.
- He may also communicate in scripture verse, or sometimes through His creatures.
- You gain a deep, inner feeling of peaceful contentment.

When you are in the presence of God, all is well.

CHAPTER II

The Purpose and Importance of Conversing with God

God Speaks through Nature

*Let the risen Jesus enter your life — welcome him as a friend…
Trust him, be confident that he is close to you,
he is with you, and he will give you the peace you are looking for
and the strength to live as he would have you do.*

–Pope Francis, The Church of Mercy[1]

The Purpose of Conversing with God Is to Know Him and Become His Friend
God Desires a Relationship with You

I never expected to befriend God, yet I believe He desires my friendship. He wants to be a part of my life — the life He created for me with Him — and I yearn for that relationship.

Before I discovered God in Nature, however, I had always struggled with loving Him, because I could not feel this love. I could only say it in words, proclaim it through liturgy, and confirm it in action.

But in Nature,
> I can sense His sweetness, if I am still.
> I can see His wonder, if I look.
> I am immersed in His magnificence, if I believe.
> And I can *feel* His love, if I open my heart.

Creation reveals God's attributes, qualities, and strengths — the evidence of His love and majesty. I can relish His richness placed in a flower; delight in His nobility in the trees swaying in the breeze; and cherish His greatness in the grandeur of the mountains and valleys. I savor the vastness of His sky — blue and white or gray, home of birds and clouds, origin of rain and snow, artists' palette for rainbows, sunsets, and dawns.

I love Nature — God's mystery. Therefore, I love *Him* when I enjoy Nature.

Is it any wonder that the prophet Isaiah's famous description of God (Isaiah 9:5) — sung in Handel's *Messiah* — has endured for nearly four decades and is proclaimed every Christmas season across the globe?

> "And His name shall be called
> Wonderful,
> Counsellor,
> the Mighty God,
> the Everlasting Father,
> the Prince of Peace."

What a Friend!

Knowing What God Wants of You
Jesus Teaches Us through Parables about Nature

When we look with new eyes at this incredible gift of creation,
we can find the sacred in the ordinary, the miracle in the mundane,
and the promise of healing in each day — each extraordinary and holy day.
–Becca Stevens of Thistle Farms, *Love Heals*[2]

How can you live God's plan for your life if you don't know what it is? And how can you learn what He has planned for you, if you don't ask Him?

While walking this Earth, Jesus used Nature parables to teach His disciples. He spoke of the mustard seed and had dealings with a fig tree; He told stories of sheep and shepherds; farmers and seeds and harvests; sparrows and weeds.

We can understand these tangible tales that teach us an intangible; examples from ordinary life that bring us into spiritual life; something close at hand that brings us closer to Him.

Creation is full of parables, and He is waiting to teach us. Through Nature, God reveals so much about Himself — but we must pause, look, and *listen*.

Reflections in this book will help you learn to apply the lessons of Nature to your life. One day, God may draw your attention to a flower of particular beauty. Ask Him what He wants you to gain through this colorful bloom. He might suggest that you notice the beautiful colors of people around you. Maybe He sends a small creature your way — a busy bee or scurrying squirrel. Perhaps He is urging you to put away your busyness and have some fun today. Through a gathering of insects sharing space and nectar, God may be asking you to do just that — share your space and nourishment with someone who needs it.

Blessings and lessons abound in creation. Remember to ask God what His special message is for you, then listen to His loving voice.

It's about Time
A Moment, a Thought, a Deed

Mental prayer in my opinion is nothing else than an intimate sharing between friends;
it means taking time frequently to be alone with Him who we know loves us.
The important thing is not to think much but to love much
and so do that which best stirs you to love.

–Saint Teresa of Avila[3]

Dedicate a bit of time each day in silence, in God's light — spending time with the One Who loves you.

- Sit quietly, take a stroll, or ride in the car — and observe.
- Silence your mind, still your heart, close your eyes and breathe.
- Contemplate your little view of creation. Wonder about it.
- Ask God or Jesus or our heavenly Mother about it — they already know what they want you to discover.
- Whatever comes to mind is your seed for the day.
- Take the tiny seed that you glean from your pondering of creation and carry it forward into your daily routine.
- Water it with the intention to be loving and gentle with each person you will encounter.
- Connect your activities to that tiny "seed of grace," nurturing it throughout the day to flourish.
- Then, you will be praying all day long, as Saint Paul urges in Ephesians 6:18: "With all prayer and supplication, pray at every opportunity in the Spirit."

Inspirational Organization to Help You along Your Journey
Trust the Seasons to Guide You

He causes the changes of the times and seasons…
He gives wisdom to the wise and knowledge to those who understand.
He reveals deep and hidden things
and knows what is in the darkness, for the light dwells with him.
–Daniel 2:21, 22

The four seasons inspire the organization of this collection of poetic readings because they are forever entwined with our own existence. Each guides us through

The Purpose and Importance of Conversing with God

the seasons of our lives, offering the wisdom of God along the way. Then, just in case we missed something, they begin again — to reveal unknown mysteries — to enrich our lives a little more, to inspire us to new discovery.

My seasons are divided by months, rather than solstices and equinoxes. So, spring includes March, April, May; summer starts at the beginning of June, and so on. This configuration may have displaced a few flowers, but I hope you won't mind.

Following the garden path, you may:

- Start at the beginning and journey through the seasons
- Select a title from the Table of Contents that intrigues you
- Skip around at your heart's desire. I trust you. It's your heart.

Write on journal pages that speak uniquely to you and revisit them as often as you like — throughout the day, week, or season — and follow *your* garden path.

Included in these pages, you will find dozens of reflections and guided contemplation to carry you through the seasons. There is no time constraint; prayer cannot be hurried — only offered in *this* eternal moment. So, you can spend a few days or even a week with a meaningful reflective thought.

As an example, you may read "God's Calling" and decide you would like to follow this inspiration every day for a week, focusing on listening to the sounds of Nature each morning, upon wakening, hearing the voice of God and His message for you.

I hope this book encourages you to enter the garden, leaving the noise of life behind and listening for the Voice of God, your friend. Begin an adventure through the four seasons into the sublime to discover God's presence in the mystery of Nature.

Come!

Journey through the Seasons
Search for God's presence in the garden
Find Him in the intricacies of Nature
Discover Him in brief encounters with His creatures
Grow with Him in grace and wisdom
Reflect on His lavish use of color in
His celestial cathedral on Earth

Now, listen to God's personal invitation to *you*

Song of Love

"Come then, my love,
my lovely one, come!
For see, winter is past,
the rains are over and gone
The flowers appear on the earth.
The season of glad songs has come,
the cooing of the turtledove is heard
in our land.
The fig tree is forming its first figs
and the blossoming vines give out their fragrance.
"Come then, my love,
my lovely one, come!"
My dove, hiding in the clefts of the rock,
in the coverts of the cliff,
show me your face,
let me hear your voice;
for your voice is sweet
and your face is beautiful."

–Song of Songs 2:10-14
Jerusalem Bible[4]

PART II

Make Your Divine Connection through

Four Seasons of Inspiration
Quotes and Scripture Verses
Reflective Poems
Gentle Prayer Guide
Journal

Your Journey Begins

*"I have seen the Lord!" she announced.
Then she reported what he had said to her.*

John 20:18

Mary Magdalen mistook Jesus for a gardener, until
He spoke and revealed Himself to her.

Do you mistake the mysteries of Nature
for something other than the revelation of God on Earth?
Enter your "garden"
then follow God's voice as He reveals Himself to you.

Spring Renewal
Growing in the Spirit in God's Garden

An Invitation

God calls to us — each of us — to come to Him
in the beauty around us
in the garden
through windows and doors
in vibrant and soft colors
in the song of the bird
in the swaying of branches
in the expanse of the firmament
in the glorious ebb and flow of everyday life!
He calls you.
He waits for you.
You.

*If every tiny flower wanted to be a rose,
spring would lose its loveliness.*
–Saint Therese Lisieux[1]

WHAT BRINGS ME TO THIS PLACE?

This place of peace.
    This place of beauty and calm.
        This place of music where Nature's melody
            and humanity's overlap in harmony —
                birds, people, dogs, vehicles.

This place where mankind's dominance over Nature —
    an airplane streaming across the sky —
        and our inability to understand the tiniest truths
            come together.

The truths of spring — the multiplicity of the tulips each year,
    the emergence of last year's flowers from seemingly barren earth,
        the blossoming of the money tree flower,
            the delicacy of color in the mounding phlox,
                the clematis clump's vivid display,
                    the budding of trees and shrubs.

This is the place where I can find God —
    in His creation — a reflection of Himself.
        If I look closely enough
            and listen carefully,
                I can hear His voice
                    in the stillness
                        in the garden.

There is always this correspondence in the Bible
between the whole world and the destiny of man…
–Blaise Arminjon, S.J., The Cantata of Love[2]

Spring Renewal

REFLECT

Can I see God in Nature? Can I envision Him in my garden space?
What is He trying to show me?
I will record descriptions of clear images so that I can hold onto them.

SEED OF GRACE

What brings us to this place?
God's presence.
Be still and listen for His voice,
contemplating His message to you,
and how it relates to your destiny.

HEAVENLY HAVEN

God began the story of our lives in a garden
The Garden of Eden
Beauty and promise
A Terrestrial Paradise
A garden of stunning beauty
Calm, restful, and safe
Blessed with pure joy and contentment
Free of worry and conflict

Where peace reigned
Where love flowed.
So, God created Man — the first man
To share in the wonder of His creation.

Man lived in God's presence
Able to hear God and speak to Him
The Almighty listened and spoke to Adam
They were bound in a sacred relationship

This was God's plan for humanity
To be in communion with Him
Forever
In the Garden.

They heard the sound of the Lord God walking about in the garden at the breezy time of the day…
Genesis 3:8

Spring Renewal

REFLECT

Today, I will find a garden and contemplate
the beginning of human life in the Garden of Eden.
I will access Nature and be still.
I will enjoy God's beauty here and feel His love.
I will sit in His presence and speak to Him.

SEED OF GRACE

Take the garden path to Divine Presence and begin
a forever friendship with God.
Start today.

GOD'S CALLING

Today, I awoke to the call of a single dove.

I looked out the window to find it perched on a roof peak, alone.
    Where is its mate? They seem to be always together.
        He calls
            gently entreating,
                every few seconds,
                      never relenting.

After a time, I hear the same persistent call, distantly.
    He has moved to a farther location in hopes of arousing the one he loves.
        His call is constant,
             but not obtrusive.
                Soft, but sure.
                    I can ignore it
                        if I choose.

This is how God calls me — gently, constantly.
    And no matter how far away I stray, He follows me, never giving up —
        for He loves me.
           I hear this in the
                call of the dove.

The song of the dove is heard in our land.
Song of Songs 2:12

REFLECT

My life is crowded, yet void.
I need to be reminded that God speaks in subtle ways
and I sometimes don't recognize His voice.
Teach me, Lord, to listen for your voice.

SEED OF GRACE

Your heart must be silent and still to hear God's voice.
He's calling you about your calling — your vocation.
Is there anything more important?
If your day is not grounded in His guidance, you will be like the lost dove.
Find a quiet moment and listen. He is waiting to speak to you.

COLD, HARD COMFORT

I sit on my front stoop.
It's cold and hard
though I don't notice it
much.

It's one of my favorite places
and I often eat my breakfast here.
I have comfy chairs elsewhere
but there is something about
this place.

It's secluded.
Quiet.

Softness in the swaying of the maple branches
Sweetness in the Japanese dogwood
Greatness in the magnificent fir.

I feel God's shelter here.
I don't need a soft chair
or travel to far-off places.
I don't need anything
more.

For He is here —
in "Our Garden."

I am with Him in
this place.

You are my refuge and shield; in your word I hope.
Psalm 119:114

REFLECT

I must find those places where I encounter
Your presence, O God.
Then, my connection with you deepens.
Thank You for special places of refuge.

SEED OF GRACE

Where do you find your inner peace?
Where do you find God's shelter from the storm?
Locate a quiet corner where you can talk to God on a daily basis
as if nothing else exists.
Take some time to be with Him in your own sacred place.

"LIVE FOREVER"

My sedum grows its leaves in tiny round-shaped clusters, close to the ground.

This morning as I was clearing away last year's stalks
in preparation for new spring growth,
I noticed the morning's dew collected within each cluster.
It was already close to noon, and the little puddles were still there,
tucked in the crevices.
I thought about how the plant would slowly "drink" the dew,
making it last throughout the day.

I had already been to Mass and Communion earlier,
and received abundant grace.
Usually, as I tumble into my daily activities,
I forget that I still have access to God's help throughout the day
whenever I need it.
I must remember to drink in slowly,
like the sedum…and then I too can
Live Forever.

*The water I shall give will become in him a
spring of water welling up to eternal life.*
John 4:14

REFLECT

I must remember to Whom I belong, and that I will live forever with Him. I ponder "Give us this day our daily bread…" as I pray "The Our Father," and what it means in my upcoming day.

SEED OF GRACE

God knows how much your soul is thirsting for a deeper relationship with Him. Today, allow His graces to overflow into your spirit with hopes of gaining eternal salvation.

COMMUNITY

Aah, the tulips in spring!
They press up through the earth even when snow covers the ground.
They multiply themselves from the previous year,
renewing annually this miracle for my spirit.

Every new season,
    I think they are too crowded and
        each slender stem will be unable to
            produce its fruit — a beautiful flower.

I vow to split them before next year,
    thinking I waited too long and
        should have already
            tended to their spacing.

Yet, each flowering season proves me wrong
    when they grace my garden with abundantly full
        clusters of brilliance and coloration.

They seem to draw their strength from
    the throng of shoots at their base,
        then reach up and spread out to
            shine with glory.

Their individual magnificence always astounds me.
    I could look closely at one and be satisfied,
        but one tulip in my garden would hardly be noticed.

So, they share nourishment at their roots to increase their numbers.
    They don't worry about overcrowdedness.
        They don't wish for more.
            They share and thrive.

Spring Renewal

Sometimes I feel stifled by people congesting my life.
    I want more space, some solitude, a little peace and quiet.
        But my lesson is learned in the spring —
            when the community of tulips displays its wisdom.

I realize I, too, must draw strength from my cluster of family and friends,
and that true individuality thrives in the midst of a community.

Finally, all of you, be of one mind,
sympathetic, loving toward one another,
compassionate, humble.
1 Peter 3:8

REFLECT

My human nature thrives on harmonious gatherings with people.
How might I encourage charitable reactions in myself and others?
Will I step aside and let another shine?
How can I respond always in kindness?
Contemplating my actions will help me to
personify commitment to community,
like the tulips.

SEED OF GRACE

Nurture the thought that there is room enough for each of us to flower
and reflect His sweet splendor, just like the single tulip. Imagine
wonderful ways to flourish within your own life's groupings —
at home with family, at work with colleagues, or in society.
Ponder how it will feel to keep your uniqueness
within their midst without causing discord.

SAINT PATRICK'S DAY

March seventeenth,
the first day to sit outside.
Temperatures are warming,
the sun is shining and
the breeze is balmy.

I am waiting for spring,
           as if it will come on a particular day,
                      all of a sudden,
                                and then, be here.

But I realize,
as I sit among my blossoming crocuses,
budding daffodils and
sprouting tulips, buttercups, and daisies,
that it is here, now.
All around.
Coursing into trunks and stems and leaves.

It's coming.
Now.
Gradually.
I can't hear it, but I can feel it —
reviving my spirit with anticipation;
filling my world with signs of new life;
preparing to bring me great joy
as it continues evolving.

Now,
        there are only glimmers of loveliness,
                only a hint of the joy that is promised,
                        when all is in full bloom...

Connecting with God in the Garden

God is like the arriving of spring —
He is here, with me, now —
Orchestrating many things in the garden of my life

to lift my spirit,
refresh me, and
prepare me
for the Great Joy that awaits me
in His Heavenly Garden.

He is here. With me. Now.

*It was one of those March days when
the sun shines hot and the wind blows cold:
when it is summer in the light and winter in the shade.*
–Charles Dickens, *Great Expectations*[4]

REFLECT

I will take God with me into my day.
Now.

SEED OF GRACE

How does spring refresh your life?
Today, keep God close to you,
listening for His voice and feeling His grace coursing through your spirit.
Give thanks to the Creator of spring!

UNDOER OF KNOTS

As my clematis rediscovers itself in new spring growth,
it is eager to climb and clasp,
tangling itself in curly knots
around anything close by,
looking for support in its upward climb.

Without gentle guidance, it becomes a clematis clump,
So, mercifully, I tend it.
I unwind its snarls, freeing it to grow to greater heights.

I, too, hold fast — to sin — becoming entangled in hopelessness,
but I cannot undo my own knots.

Come to my aid, Mother of Fair Love,
with your gentle, loving fingers.
Unwind the tendrils of my life
freeing me to love as Christ loves.

*The knot of Eve's disobedience was untied by
Mary's obedience: what the virgin Eve bound
through her disbelief, Mary loosened by her faith.*
    –Saint Irenaeus[5]

REFLECT

Blessed Lady, gently guide me today.
Detangle the knots of my flaws and failings
so that I may aspire to greater heights.

SEED OF GRACE

Ask Mary, your heavenly Mother, to help you in your day.
Be specific and anticipate her help, for she never refuses her child.

REJUVENATING RAIN

It begins.
Tiny wonders — raindrops.
The smell — fresh and distinct — unlike anything else.
Exhilarating breaths

It increases.
Immense richness — downpour.
The sound — rushing water — not like falling drops.
It is one vast, immeasurable splendor — like God.

The breeze — fresh and strong — invigorating.
Deep breaths

A thousand tiny drops — a million.
A trillion tiny drops sent from the heavens as one rain to
    Cleanse
        Refresh
            Renew
                Drench
                    Quench
                        Revive
                            Rejuvenate

This is how we know God
First in tiny droplets of devotion — ours given to Him,
and then in boundless abundance — His blessings bestowed upon us.
quiet s i g h s

*He gave you rains from heaven and fruitful seasons,
and filled you with nourishment and gladness for your hearts.*
Acts of the Apostles 14:17

Spring Renewal

REFLECT

Lord, I long for Your cleansing refreshment!

What droplets of love can I give you in return?
I will rejoice in Your richness and
revive my thankfulness for all Your blessings.

SEED OF GRACE

Where will you feel the rejuvenation of God's grace?
Why not refresh yourself today, spellbound by Nature?
Consider stepping out in the cleansing rain to feel
God's majestic gift and give thanks.

PERFECT SERENITY

I stand under trees in my garden
in a sprinkle of rain.
I wonder not why
Jesus prayed in the garden.

Scent of fresh rain
Breath of spring

A robin on a tree branch
enjoys himself.
I wonder why
he's here, unsheltered.

Nature surrounds
Silence inspires awe

Today is Good Friday,
Jesus prayed in the garden.

*There was a garden there, and he
and his disciples entered it.*
John 18:1

Spring Renewal

REFLECT

The joy and serenity in the garden are a stark contrast to the agony and sorrow that Jesus experienced there. He died that I might live.
He suffered that I may be healed.
The great exchange of the Cross — His life for mine.

SEED OF GRACE

It is no wonder that Jesus went to the garden to pray in His agony.
He found comfort in His creation: nature, angels, the night,
and even His sleeping apostles nearby.
You will meet Him there, if you go.

LIFTING FOR LOVE

The ant lifts the crumb
   twice its size
      and struggles to drag it.
Where?

Sunrise lifts the fog
   clearing the sky
      obliterating blur.
How?

Humankind lifts from bed
   with purpose anew
      anticipating the day.
For what?

The God-Man hoists His heavy tree
   thrice His size
      struggling to drag it.
Why?

The Son lifts the log
   clearing our way
      anticipating our day
For love.

Lord, teach me to be generous…to give and not count the cost
      –Saint Ignatius of Loyola[6]

Spring Renewal

REFLECT

As I tumble out of bed every morning and follow my routine,
do I know the reason? Do I consider my purpose?
God bestowed this new awakening upon me. What a gift!
I need to think of a favor I can do for Him today.
I will embrace my struggles
for love.

SEED OF GRACE

What will you lift today, embracing the struggle, to clear the fog, for love?

BIRDS OF PEACE

A nest of doves is hidden in the lush lower branches of my tree.
I come upon it suddenly one day while trimming.
I startle as much as mother dove.
Yet, she doesn't flinch, doesn't "say a word."
I quietly speak an apology to her and move gently away.

A mother robin could not have remained —
she would have squawked at me and flown elsewhere,
leaving her eggs unprotected.
She would have scolded me from afar
in an attempt to lure me from her precious ones.

But the dove is quiet, serene, and still.

Weeks later, the babies explore the yard.
They, too, are calm — secure in their surroundings,
basking in the sun.
If I approach too closely,
they flutter a few feet away, making room for me
rather than escaping my invasion.

Perhaps these characteristics have earned them their title:
Birds of Peace.
I can learn from them —
no squawking, stay calm, no sudden reactions.
Face my aggressor.

Truly, they must know
the presence of God.

Dismiss all anxiety from your minds.
Philippians 4:6

Spring Renewal

REFLECT

When can I practice composure?
What moments am I prone to interject?
What circumstances agitate me and how can I give a tranquil response?

SEED OF GRACE

This mother dove is reminiscent of the quiet, gentle Mother of God,
whom poets refer to as the "woman wrapped in silence."
Today, nurture peace in moments of agitation,
asking her to wrap you in her mantle.

DIVINE DESIGN

My garden plans are definite.
I know exactly what annuals I want,
where I will place them and
which store offers the best quality.
I know this from many years of planning and planting.

Arriving at the store, however,
I may not find the right colors,
or even the particular flower I desire.
So, I alter my arrangement.

While I'm planting,
I change my mind —
this looks better over there and maybe a pot over here.
Again, I fine-tune my flower-scape.

When I finish,
although a garden is never finished,
it is heavenly —
better than my original vision.

This is how God guides the course of my life —
gradually, gracefully
through seemingly chance choices,
daily, annually, perennially.
If I accept His deviation of design, in the end it is always better.
God crafts my life with loving care.

Trust in the Lord with all your heart, on your own intelligence do not rely;
In all your ways be mindful of him, and he will make straight your paths.

Proverbs 3:5-6

Spring Renewal

REFLECT

Recalling a recent alteration to my plans,
I realize that the change made things better than expected.
I am grateful to you, O Lord, for managing my life.

SEED OF GRACE

Make plans, but open your heart to changes that come along —
the Holy Spirit directing the course of your life and those around you.
Today, try to discern where changes might arise
and be open to the improved version.

WEEDS

The morning sun shone on
the climbing clematis drooping over
the fence above
the creeping phlox.

The colors were magnificent —
vivid cerise flowing down upon
subtle pastel purple.

The scene was captivating
The light was perfect
I thought about taking a picture.
(Indecisiveness)

The moment passed
I let it go —
"I'll have tomorrow."
(Procrastination)

The chance never came.
There were clouds
then rain
and inopportunity.
(Busyness)

The phlox in its last days of fruition
diminished under the hand of the elements —
blossoms faded and lost.
The perfect moment passed.

The "weeds" of my existence
overpowered the gift set before me.
If I resist busyness,
act upon firm decisions,
and cast aside procrastination,
I could be immersed in perfect moments
celebrating an abundant life!

Without hard work nothing grows but weeds.
–Gordon B. Hinckley[7]

REFLECT

Imagine what I could accomplish and enjoy without weeds filling my day.
What weeds can I remove from my life?
I will write them down and leave them behind.

SEED OF GRACE

Sometimes it's hard to tell what is a weed and what is a flower.
Sometimes you have to wait and see if it blooms.
Maybe God is waiting for you to ask the question
so He can speak to you.

SILENT BEAUTY

I bought petunias of two colors: one yellow,
as soft and subtle as the early morning,
and one magenta,
deep and rich, like the evening sky.

I chose them separately for their
individual attributes.
Until…I set them on my low brick wall together
awaiting their final resting place in my garden.

How they complement each other is striking.
Intriguing.
My eyes are continually drawn to their quiet resolve.
To look at them brings satisfaction,
peace.

Separating them seems impossible now.
Each would be less without the other.
I must find a place to plant them,
next to each other.

Likewise, I must live
side by side, peacefully, with my spouse,
different but alike, completing each other;
presenting a genuine unity for all to see.

*Come, my Beloved, Let us go to the fields…We will see if the vines are budding,
if their blossoms are opening, if the pomegranate trees are in flower.
Then I shall give you the gift of my love.*
–Blaise Arminjon, S.J., *The Cantata of Love*[8]

Spring Renewal

REFLECT
The Sacrament of Marriage creates a sum
greater than its parts, a unified whole.
A complementarity.
A richness that presents a divine paradox.
What is God trying to tell me within my marriage?
Listen. Can I hear Him in the voice of my spouse?

SEED OF GRACE
Ponder these gentle virtues of the petunias regarding relationships:
Nurture your unique gifts, connect with complements,
possess quiet resolve, remain committed.
The greatest of these is love.
Think about the relationships you will encounter today.

HIDDEN AZALEA

Years ago, the azalea — a gift at the birth of my last-born son — was planted.
I didn't know it needed specific nourishment — special soil,
so, it struggled among its family of flowers.

Through the years the other plantings in the bed flourished.
The phlox crept in, day lilies encroached, and
strawberries all but covered up this lowly little azalea.

Still, it did its best —
sending a few lovely vivid flowers every spring.

Its space overwhelmed by surrounding growth;
its allure outshone by prolific blossoms —
it was hardly noticed except to knowing eyes.

I am like the hidden azalea:
    yearning for a better environment,
        wishing for more space,
            or nourishment for my needs.

I am like a hidden azalea:
    "important" work being done all around,
        tending my "small" life — domestic duties,
            modest job, nurturing, caring, being.

Sometimes I want to be noticed.
Still, I do my best — sending my lovely, delicate flowers — never hidden from the Son.

*There is comfort in faith, and warmth in hope, but when we continue to love
when these seem to be gone and there is but a thread to hang on to — then
we truly love, then His purifying silence has completed its work;
we have risen to a new level of union; we have climbed another mountain.*
–Mother Angelica[9]

REFLECT

As I look at my azalea, I feel at one with this delicate shrub, unseen, hiding from God.
He urges me to come out, to see Him, to hear His voice,
to glorify Him through the gracefulness He bestowed upon me —
An elegance He sees even when I feel bereft of blossoms.

SEED OF GRACE

Jesus came to Earth to teach us by example, and for most of His life,
He lived an obscure existence in humility
and earnestness, alongside Joseph and Mary.
Today, endeavor to emulate this model of holiness and happiness.

DEW POINT

    Today the dew is profuse —
        clinging to the low limbs of the
            redbud tree on the boulevard, waiting to let go,
                quench its roots and be drawn up again;
                    weighing down branches of Mary's "hover bush"
                        and sparkling the green lawn.
    Delicate condensation covers my porch
            refreshing my potted plant
                and dampening my chair.
    Sumptuous moisture drips
        from leaves
            from petals
                from the end of the wrought iron curlicue
                    onto the ground
                        into the Earth
                          saturating its very core.

Bounteous droplets seem to ooze from the atmosphere.
Everything is fresh, renewed, excited, and alive.
Pure life-giving water is the *essence* — not the trees, not the grass, not the plants.

Like God's grace
Everywhere
Clinging, refreshing, renewing
Abundant
I yearn to be filled
Cling to me!

Saturate my day, Mediatrix of all grace. Walk with me in the dew of Heaven.
Freshen my day with His grace, the essence of His presence.
Renew my soul with this gift and I will ask for more when my dew point is low.

                Behold, I make all things new.
                    Revelation 21:5

REFLECT

When my reservoirs run low, what can I do to replenish God's glory?
With God's grace I can embrace each day with joy as a new beginning
and opportunity for a fresh start.

SEED OF GRACE

Connect with God's glorious Circle of Life, like the morning dew!
His grace is close and ever-present.

MAGNIFICENT MAPLE

Whirligigs everywhere in spring
Abundance

Cooling shade in summer's heat
Kindness

Lush, lofty leafy-ness
Graciousness

Birds' bounty, squirrels' playground
Hospitality

A sense of wonder and awe
Magnificence!

Branches spreading across and beyond
        the entire expanse of lawn, over the garage and
                into the neighboring yard,
    the Maple shares its nature.
     Unconditional Love

Impressive virtues freely given by a lesser creature than I.
Many lessons to learn from this Magnificent Maple.

For this very reason, make every effort to supplement your faith with virtue…
2 Peter 1:5

REFLECT

Can I love completely?
Do I tell those I love often enough?
Do they feel my unconditional love?

SEED OF GRACE

Is God asking you to spread your branches?
Do you have enough virtue to extend yourself?
Choose your favorite Magnificent Maple virtue
and nurture it in your connections today.

THOUGHTS ON A DAY IN MAY
by Anne A. Imperi

The day was too beautiful to hold.
May,
with all its promise and new hope, burst with joy upon the morning.
The goodness of God had overflowed into His creation with
such an extravagance of sound and color this morning
that the human heart could hardly contain it.

I thought about that.
How small we stand in the midst of nature's beauty,
trying to hold in our heart just one glorious day at a time.
How small the human heart!
How small the human mind as it tries to
contemplate the mind of God,
from Whom all goodness and beauty come.

The human artist spends a lifetime striving to capture
a bit of the world's beauty on canvas or in words or with music,
a beauty and grandeur forever showing itself in new and endless variety.
Or perhaps he probes the soul of that most noble —
and ignoble — of God's creation,
Man,
reflecting nature's recurring truths;
the inevitability of death and the miracle of rebirth.

Occasionally, the world is awed by the art of
a Michelangelo, a Bach or a Shakespeare.
It lauds their great genius and marvels
at what their imagination and skill have "created."
But put together with all the art of history,
yesterday and tomorrow, it is still no more than
a small part of the Universe and of what, in its entirety,
is but a flick of the brush to the Divine Artist!

Spring Renewal

If the greatest of men struggle to reproduce
this tiny fraction of the beauty and truth which is God,
how can we not but wonder at such a mystery,
and regret our sometimes-ho-hum familiarity with Him,
the Lord of the Universe, Who has surrounded us with all this
evidence of His love and power?

Instead, we continue to take credit for what is not ours.
It is no wonder God hides Himself from us,
showing us just His signs in the world and waiting for us to recognize them.
The delight of this May day then becomes
a taste of the indescribable sweetness of His Presence.

God is an artist, and the universe is His work of art.
—Saint Thomas Aquinas [11]

When I began writing this collection of seasonal reflections, I did not know my mother enjoyed the same wonder of God's creation as I do. Because she is a writer, I began sharing them with her for advice. One day, I received an envelope in the mail, containing "Thoughts on a Day in May," which had been tucked away for several years. I share it with you in celebration of her 100th year.

Journey Into Summer

*His divine power has bestowed on us everything
that makes for life and devotion,
through the knowledge of him who called us
by his own glory and power.*
2 Peter 1:3

Summer — abundant with fruits, flowers and fragrance, creatures and creation!
Continue to follow God's beckoning for an inspiriting adventure,
refreshed by God's breath in a summer breeze,
visited by birds and butterflies,
calmed by pleasant scents and sounds,
and invigorated by gentle rain and morning dew —
God's Living Waters.

Summer Ease
Praying Effortlessly in God's Garden

Find the Spirit!

When my children were young,
we would welcome a refreshing breeze on a hot summer's day with:
"Aah…the Holy Spirit!
We would pause and face Him,
spreading wide our arms to capture as much as we could of the gentle gust,
and wait for Him.
Still to this day,
the movement of trees in the breeze enraptures me.
Praying can be this easy:
Simply, open your arms and open your heart.

*God…comes to us in the light breeze,
that never imposes itself,
but asks to be heard.*
—Pope Francis[1]

SUMMER VACATION

I glance out the back door
        Buttercups flutter in the breeze
There's a delightful tinkling from wind chimes
        Tree branches totter and sway
Birds chirp here and there
        I step out

My posture lifts with the breeze
        My hair gives way
I stand, becoming
      a part of the breeze's
           dance.
                I think,
                    this is like
                          the ocean
                                I need not go there —
        shrubs and tree branches alike
                caught in the ebb and flow
                      of my backyard.

                      Aah! even the sea has not my
                beautiful buttercups
            radiant roses
          pleasing petunias
        climbing clematis.

I step forward
        my bare feet caress the grass
no need for sand
        The sun shimmers on the yellows
through the greens and
        beyond into the distance
no need for rippling water

      My yard has its own tides
              they beckon

His is the sea, for he has made it, and the dry land, which his hands have formed.
                Psalm 95:5

Summer Ease

REFLECT

I always long for the ocean and wish for a chance to go each year.
Yet, standing at my back door, I revel in the blessings God sends
in a summer breeze and bare-feet grass with rippling tides!
Creation at its most wondrous! An ocean of possibilities.

SEED OF GRACE

You needn't travel to faraway places, nor venture distantly
to experience God's beauty in Nature and its surroundings,
which provide enjoyment and serenity in your life.
Thank the Lord for summer, and tell Him some of your favorite joys.

MINIATURE ROSE

I sit near my miniature rose bush —
soft, delicate, pastel pink buds opening to small flowers of pure white petals.
This petite shrub displays all stages of development simultaneously:
some wilting, some budding and some blossoming.
From my perch,
I notice a singular rose in full bloom,
too heavy for its supporting stem —
gracefully arching over, looking at the ground,
hidden from the sun, and me.
I reach down,
gently propping it up against a stronger stem
taking this opportunity to lean over
and enjoy its fragrance.

It takes my breath away
It swells my soul
It permeates my senses!
I am compelled to remain for a few more breaths.

I return to my seat, glancing at its delicacy which captures my eye
as much as its perfume engaged my nose.

Gazing, I ponder its elegance within my heart.

My rose is like the "Little Flower"
hidden in cloister, unseen by the world
and yet still sending sweet perfume and
Showers of Roses
to those who will notice and
bend down in prayer.

What do you say to Jesus? "I don't say anything. I love Him."
–Saint Therese Lisieux, "The Little Flower"[2]

Summer Ease

REFLECT

The size and shape of this singular, pure white miniature rose
brings to mind Jesus in the Eucharist.
Dear Jesus, never let me lose sight of You
and support me in finding Your presence everywhere,
and taking in Your divine fragrance.

SEED OF GRACE

Saint Therese proclaimed,
"I have only to cast a glance in the Gospels and immediately
I breathe in the perfumes of Jesus' life."[3]
Read some scripture in the garden with her
and ask her to shower your day with sweet fragrances.

PEACEFUL SUNDAY

I sit amidst my buttercups.
The yellow, vibrantly shimmering in the sun,
still gleams in the shadow of a cloud passing over.
Bright petals beside me are in definite detail,
those beyond, a sea of blurred brilliance.
Leaves quiver as a gentle breeze of God's breath drifts through.

Roses nearby — pale, pastel pink miniatures, almost white;
vivid rose-colored — nearly red, but not quite.
The clematis too — deep purple velvet.
These beauties — a backdrop for the buttercups' more-than-yellow yellow.

Bird songs enhance the peace, like sacred hymns;
even the distant hum of a lawn mower does not intrude.
This is Sunday.
God's day.
Isn't it obvious?

*God blessed the seventh day and made it holy,
because on it he rested from all the
work he had done in creation.*
Genesis 2:3

REFLECT

Sometimes my Sunday is a day for catch up,
when instead I need to relax and rest;
a good day to contemplate God in Nature,
asking Him questions and listening to His voice.

SEED OF GRACE

We all have a lot of work to do, just as God did in creation.
We all need a rest, and He has provided the prescribed time — Sunday.
His day.
The day He made holy.
Rest. And give it back to Him.
Enjoy the peace.

YESTERDAY AND TODAY

I sit in the gray morning and notice the day lilies of yesterday.
Their blossoms are closed.
I knew they would be,
for they have only one day
to shimmer in the sunlight.

I don't mind this,
because their "sisters" will brighten
my garden and my life the next day.
And sometimes I forget that they, themselves, are gone.

But today is overcast, and will show no new flowers.
The sisters have no reason to open their petals to the world,
for there is no sun to enhance their charm.
So, they will wait.

Maybe I will see them tomorrow.
Today I enjoy only the memory of yesterday's blossoms
and what they left behind:
delicately curving peach-colored lines.

Yesterday
was their day to shine.
To share with the world
all they had to give.

I wonder

What brilliance could I show
without the Son,
the Divine Son?
He has given me this day to glisten in His light.

Summer Ease

What will I share with my world today?
What influence will I give to my sisters and brothers
so they can shine tomorrow,
when I am gone?

*Yesterday is gone, tomorrow has not yet come.
We have only today, let us begin.*
–Saint Teresa of Calcutta[4]

REFLECT

What will I leave behind?
Will I leave delicate lines to suggest my past brilliance?
Today, I resolve to share my beauty with the world —
my family, neighbors, friends, and strangers —
for, like this lily, today is all I have.

SEED OF GRACE

"Life is the flash of a firefly in the night, the breath of a buffalo
in the wintertime, and the little shadow which runs
across the grass and loses itself in the sunset."[5]
Consider this Native American proverb from long ago and
determine how you will manage your time.
Today.

GRACEFULNESS IN ORDER

If God is in Nature, then what does a cornfield tell me about Him?

What attributes of the field reflect God's?
Order and grace come to mind.

Rows and rows standing so uniformly,
Grass mown at the edges so neatly,
Breeze touching the leaves ever so gently,
causing them to ripple gracefully like the ruffling of water —
an enormously magnificent picture of order and grace joined together.

Childhood memories —
traveling from West Virginia to Michigan
on two-lane highways,
counting farm animals to overcome boredom.

Aah, then the cornfields!
They had a magical lure.
They were pleasurable to look upon,
mesmerizing to watch
the towering, unending rows trailing by.

And now, even as an adult in central Ohio,
I pass farmland in between cities
or should I say cities in between farmland?
And, oh, when I pass a cornfield!
So restful to watch it go by.

Different from all the other rural green scenes,
cornfields stand on the sidelines,
gently presenting themselves...

They do not impose;
they are not obtrusive —
such graceful order.

The cornfield tells me about
God's gracefulness in order,
and much fruit to be harvested.
If God designed a cornfield in this fashion,
surely He will help me establish this same tranquility in my life.
I need only ask.

He is not the God of disorder but of peace.
1 Corinthians 14:33

REFLECT

Does grace encourage individual responsibility
to complete my own mission within the multitude?
Does order promote unity to stand alongside others —
one of many in harmony?

Please, dear Jesus, give me the grace to put the most important matters
in order — my relationships with You and with my loved ones.

SEED OF GRACE

Think of a place in your life where a little orderliness could produce fruit.
Then, ask God's blessing for order through gracefulness.

FIG LEAVES IN THE RAIN

Aah …
delicious gentle summer rain.
I watch as drip after drip awakens leaves everywhere.
Small leaves just jiggle in response,
but the big fig leaf is, by far, the most entertaining to watch.
Because of size and shape,
its response to each drop is
a graceful bounce,
like a dance.

Is this how God touches me?
A drop of refreshing grace,
and then another, and another
until I am sated?

How do I respond?
With a little jiggle
or do I get involved in life's dance?

I think of the barren fig tree Jesus passed by, then cursed.
If I don't accept His grace, will I too shrivel up and die?
Perhaps, this is the strong message God sends me
in the gentle summer rain.

He said to it, "May no fruit ever come from you again."
And immediately the fig tree withered.
Matthew 21:19

Summer Ease

REFLECT

The Divine Dance! God invites me into the rhythm of it —
the interaction of the Father, Son, and Holy Spirit.
Do I respond? Or am I too distracted by my own agenda?
Do I fully embrace His presence and prompting,
and engage with my whole being,
or just a passing two-step?
Today, I will turn my full attention to interact with the Holy Trinity.

SEED OF GRACE

Quietly, like a gentle summer rain, consider what awaits you
in the coming day. What is God trying to awaken in you?
How can you unfurl your leaves and welcome His gentle touch?
Listen to His voice like gentle raindrops.

GARDEN PRAYERS

Pray always.
Saint Paul says to.
How will I find the time?
There is so much to do.

I love being with God's creations in my gardens —
I will pray out here.
I will offer my garden time for someone, something.
Can I do more?

Maybe I can pray while I water:
a Hail Mary for each flower,
ten flowers, one decade of the rosary,
and my flowers get evenly watered.
That's a start.

And then
I can talk to Him:
Ask Him what He wants to do with me today
give Him my troubles and sorrows
marvel at the wonders before me
thank Him for the colors and textures of my garden, my life
tell Him how sorry I am for my transgressions
pray for those whom I have wronged
and those who have hurt me
ask for His grace and His blessings.
All these prayers He hears in my garden.

I can take this idea into the rest of my life and in this way
I can pray always as
Saint Paul recommends.

O garden-dweller, my friends are listening for your voice, let me hear it!
Song of Songs 8:13[6]

REFLECT

What is prayer?
Did Saint Paul mean to stop everything, kneel down, and say words?
Could he have meant that everything I think, do, and say is prayer?
When tending His creation, I am carrying out an act of worship —
a lovely way to pray.

SEED OF GRACE

"Pray always" doesn't mean you get nothing else done,
but that you ground your day with the intent to
include God in everything you do —
listening to His advice all the while.
Take a moment to consider how you will do this.

OUR GARDEN

I sit on my front step,
surrounded by my garden of
shrubs, flowers, trees, and grass.

I created it and designed it.
I dug, cultivated, planted, thinned, pruned, trimmed, weeded, and watered.

Is it my design of God's Creation, or my creation of God's Design?
No matter
But it is imperative that I nurture His natural world
I am the laborer, and He the Master.

And so it is with all things:
He calls me to do His work
and I must pick up the shovel and begin.

There is still much to do
so I continue
tending this beauteous place
for God and me.

Our Garden.

*Neither the one who plants nor the one who waters is anything,
but only God, who causes the growth.*
1 Corinthians 3:7

Summer Ease

REFLECT

Today, I will state my intention to do God's work — nurturing and tending.
Intentions are powerful and will help me remember my promise.
But, first, I must ask Him what He wants of me — today.
Just today.

SEED OF GRACE

Ponder joining your will with God's Will.
Remember to "take up your shovel" and try to do His work.

GOD'S FINGERPRINTS

How can I be concerned with the details of my life
when I look closely at the intricacy of the center of the coneflower?

In my garden, surrounded by God's blessings, I consider all these details:
the delicacy of the daylily,
the softness of the sweet pea
and the strength of the sedum
the long-lastingness of roses and clematis
the innocent arc of the "swan heads"
the deep green leafage of the hosta thriving in the shade;
and prolific clusters of cherry red tomatoes, each ripening in its own time.

Inspired, I vow to champion my uniqueness,
to realize that delicacy and softness are far from weakness.
I need not concern myself with my life's length or strength,
but rather be guided by its shape —
whether a simplistic existence
or laden with details.

O Lord, guide me humbly along
the innocent arc by which
You fashion my life;
let me come faithfully to fruition
in my own time;
cultivate colorful abundance
through my love of all creation;
grow in me a
heavenly landscape
so I might recognize Your fingerprints within the garden of my life.

I praise you, because I am wonderfully made…
Psalm 139:14

REFLECT

Today I will see myself as God made me — look at myself through His eyes.
What beauty and wonder will I see?
I will take a moment to thank Him for the wonderful work of art that I am.
I will contemplate some of the special gifts He gave me,
and that I, in turn, give the world.
I will keep them close to my heart.

SEED OF GRACE

Today, recognize how wonderfully you have been made!
Notice the moments when God's hands guide you.
Trust Him to bring you faithfully to fruition in your own time.
Think fondly of yourself, as He does.

GIVING AND RECEIVING

The garden phlox are always at risk in July's
intense heat and lack of rain.
Matching my height while in full bloom, they need assistance.

As I work my hose around and through the deep bed to drench their roots,
the beautiful scent enters my nose as one flower touches my nostrils.
I take a deep breath. I close my eyes and take another. And again.

Did I lean in to reach the back row?
Or did she reach out to me in gratitude?
I'm not sure,
but I am reminded by Saint Francis,
the great lover of Nature, that
"It is in giving that we receive."

As she continues drinking in the refreshment,
I take another breath of her "heaven-scent" fragrance.

He who refreshes others will himself be refreshed.
Proverbs 11:25

Summer Ease

REFLECT

"It is in giving that we receive."
So contrary to our human nature, which always wants to receive.
Today, I will focus on how I can nourish another:
a smile, a hand, a cup of water, a prayer of blessing.
There is no disappointment in giving.

SEED OF GRACE

You may never know how your mundane daily chores unexpectedly nurture others. Recall a kindness that you showed someone that you thought was inconsequential. Ponder how you might have refreshed their spirit in ways you hadn't imagined.

SUNDAY MORNING

Quiet.
No people.
No traffic.
Birds chirping.
A distant hum of
cars on the highway.

As I sit in my garden, peacefully drinking it all in, I notice a sparkling bead of dew on each tiny blade of grass. It glimmers in the sun, and glitters in the shade, too. God knew it needed that drop of moisture to survive the day's coming heat. Unsolicited, but sent, they received their "daily bread." I wonder how it came to those hiding under the low-hanging branches of the evergreen tree. God found even them.

Beyond is my hydrangea bush with upturned leaves glittering with many collected drops of dew. As I admire its charming pink blossoms of blossoms, one bead of dew, almost imperceptibly, drips off the tip of one leaf, to soak into the earth and quench her roots.

God sends cooling moisture of grace to me too, through this world of people, activities, work, and experiences. I need only to accept them. Gather them. Drink them in.

If I am wise,
like a blade of grass,
I receive my "daily dew."
If I am receptive,
like the hydrangea,
I allow the overflow of God's gifts to soak deep into my soul to nourish my life's garden.
I become one with God.

But whoever drinks the water I shall give will never thirst…
John 4:14

REFLECT

I ask for many things, but receive many more.
Today, I will pay attention to unasked-for gifts from God
and give Him thanks!

SEED OF GRACE

Virtues of the hydrangea to contemplate: receptivity, trust, surrender.
Imagine how these graces can become part of your life.
Have some of your blessings gone unnoticed?

DUTY AND SHADOWS

I took pictures today of my pot of multicolored flowers.
They glistened in the sunlight: yellow, purple, and magenta.
The blooms were stunning, reflecting the sun's light almost like water.
I thought they could not be more splendid.

Now, I sit at the table next to them in the shade, after a magnificently sunny day.
Their colors are equally as stunning —
Rich, yet subtle, soft, and soothing.
They seem confident: solid and stalwart, as if to say
"I don't need the sunlight to shine, I have worthiness of my own."

I get a good feeling about my daily duties,
when I think about this pleasing display in the shade.
I do not need the limelight of human appreciation
to make my offerings worthwhile.
When I take care of my responsibilities, whether mundane or great,
my activities may become a bouquet to shine for others to see,
or remain silent in the shadows.
Either way
I have done my part
I arranged a bouquet of life.

*The Son of Man did not come to be served but to serve
and to give his life as a ransom for many.*
Matthew 20:28

Summer Ease

REFLECT

Today, I will be open to God's grace,
listening for His advice while performing my duties.
Both are necessary to live life to the full!
Goodness brings gladness.

SEED OF GRACE

Oh, the struggles against pride — the want of appreciation.
When you feel this yearning, find a peaceful place and
ponder the humility of Nature. Like the pot of multicolored flowers,
you can be happy in bright moments as well as on dimmer days —
always a shining reflection of Jesus, the Son.

THE COLOR OF GOD

I love to look out my window at the array of color —
distinctive tints and variant hues.
So many shades of pinks
and such a variety of purples and yellows.

My garden phlox presents a display from the faintest blush of crimson to
soft periwinkle and vivid lilac
to a deep, hearty magenta —
a seamless variance of color
that one might call just "pink,"
yet each distinctly delightful.

Even more brilliant is the white phlox.
Stunning.
Pure.
Set apart from the others
not in space, but due to its stark contrast of color.
White is definitely not lacking in intensity,
for these alabaster sentinels in my garden are remarkable —
even more so than vibrant variegated shades.

Perhaps in Heaven,
we will be pinks, purples,
yellows, and reds.
God
will shine dazzling white.

His appearance was like lightning and his clothing was white as snow.
Matthew 28:3

Summer Ease

REFLECT

Like the multicolored flowers in a garden that
live seamlessly together to create beauty,
I am one of the flowers in God's Garden.
What color will I choose to be today?

SEED OF GRACE

In your search for truth, follow God's dazzling light.
He is the Way, the Truth, and the Light.
Think ahead and contemplate where
God's light might brighten your day.
Let it shine there.

ROSE OF SHARON

The Rose of Sharon boughs arch
    gracefully from the weight of its
        seed pods and few remaining flowers.

It does not seem burdened, though.
    The gentle curves of its branches create not only
        a beautiful shape as they grace my path, but also
            a feeling of quiet humility, as they bow down before me.

    Surrounded by them, I feel peace
        protected — even honored as I pass by.

        Is it any wonder, then, the Virgin Mother is called
            "Rose of Sharon"?
                — attributing qualities of this flowering shrub to her
                    for she bears our burdens with grace
                        in humble service and silent beauty.

I am a flower of Sharon.
a lily of the valleys.
Song of Songs 2:1

Summer Ease

REFLECT

I will ask this Rose for advice,
thinking of her wise grace and quiet humility of service,
which echo that of Jesus' washing the feet of His disciples.
By doing so, He shows that serving others is *not* a burden,
but rather a beautiful gift returned to the Father.

SEED OF GRACE

After last night's storm,
a Rose of Sharon sapling arches over the path to the gate,
blocking entry to the side garden. Consider what path you desire
to take today that the Mother of God wishes you would not?
Ask her.

A BUTTERFLY'S LOVE

A tiny golden-colored butterfly
alights on my hand as I water my August flowers.
I smile and ask how her morning and night have been.
She doesn't answer, but lingers, keeping me company.

As I gaze upon her upon my hand,
I move gently to dislodge her not,
for I love her tender touch upon my skin.
But more — her friendship. I want her to stay.

"A bit of advice I ask of you,
what wisdom do you share today?"
I ask hoping to detain her with conversation.
No answer does she give.
What wise advice could "Golda" give

to those of us who wish to live
otherwise?
For all she does is flit and sit.
She doesn't come with lessons learned.

And then in a flicker,
as she flutters away,
"I love you too,"
I hear myself say.

I realize in my reply
She's answered only as she knows.
She gave me wisdom from above,
for she was made to love.

Let us love, since that is all our hearts were made for.
  –Saint Therese of Lisieux[7]

Summer Ease

REFLECT

Butterflies bestow their love upon flowers through
their important role as pollinator. I wonder what a butterfly
would tell me about sharing with others.
I will listen.

SEED OF GRACE

Like all of God's creatures, butterflies do always what they were created to do.
Consider and contemplate what God created you to do.
Could it be to love?
There is your mission for today.

GOD'S TOUCH

For two months, the heat had been unbearable; the drought oppressive. My flowers had suffered even though I watered every day. Mine was a futile attempt to keep them all alive, so I decided to neglect certain beds, realizing they could never recover this season, but would return the following year.

Then the rains came.

My Faith was renewed, as were the limp and drooping perennials. Similarly, a small strip of annuals, which had not flowered in weeks, suddenly came to life and color with the heavenly moisture.

This morning, I marvel at their new vitality and fullness. How could these lifeless plants have recovered to wholeness so quickly?

I am reminded of the difference between my efforts and God's loving touch. I am also reminded that I too am perennial — I will live forever and God is just dying to assist me.

Prayer: Dear Lord, when I am withering from the day's heat, drench me with your Living Water, and restore my vigor, so that I might overcome trials and tribulations. Amen.

Then the Lord will…satisfy your thirst in parched places, will give strength…And you shall be like a watered garden…
Isaiah 58:11

REFLECT

What in my life has God touched?
I sit in my garden, listening for His voice,
and He helps me contemplate.
I ask Him where He has touched my life
and strengthened my faith, and He tells me.

SEED OF GRACE

Sit with Him in grateful praise,
remembering a time of drought in your life
when you felt God's loving touch
and were refreshed and renewed.

DANDELIONS

It's August. Dandelions are long gone — or should be.

Today, however, I notice one and hasten to pluck it out.
Coming upon it makes me pause:
Its wispy whiteness, perfect roundness, and transparent symmetry
are breathtaking.

How could this be? It's a weed,
and those in spring — white and ready to blow — did not impress me thus.
I began to think about myself and my own weedy-ness.

My past and present are so riddled with unworthiness
could there be hope?
Do I still have something to offer
even as blemished as I am?

I find my encouragement in a little weed:
This particular dandelion had
persisted through heat and drought
against all odds
to grow splendid and resilient
thriving all alone
in my garden.

This little weed inspires me
to do likewise in God's Garden —
my place in this world.
This misplaced dandelion
its natural purity of design
were heavenly crafted.
And so am I.

First collect the weeds and bundle them up to burn...
The angels will hurl them into the fiery furnace...
Matthew 13:30, 13:42

Summer Ease

REFLECT

Lord, as I listen for Your voice,
remind me in our conversation that
Your creation encompasses everything and everyone.

Every time I see symmetry, I feel as though I encounter Christ.
So, now I carefully pick the white dandelions gently placing them in a vase (no water needed).
Gorgeous! – this fabulous flower of many medicinal and nutritional benefits.

SEED OF GRACE

Think of a place in your life where
symmetry offers you tranquility and join God there.

THE REAL THING

I planted a strawberry in a pot
and the leaves grew.
I thought I'd have to wait
until next year for fruit.

But here it is, the end of August,
and I just picked five tiny strawberries.
Unable to resist tasting
I devoured the luscious fruit.

I thought they might be tart,
given their small size,
but they were delectable —
different from store varieties —
and I was satisfied.

I imagine that's how it is with Heaven.
There are glimpses on Earth in a wildflower,
a gentle breeze, a kind smile,
to help us through this life.

But when
we arrive in Heaven,
we will taste of the Real Thing.
We will be truly satisfied.
For eternity.

Taste and see how good the Lord is…
Psalm 34:9

REFLECT

My life on earth
provides a mere sampling of the Real Thing
that is to come when I reach Eternity.
I will ponder "What God has prepared for those who love him…"
(1 Corinthians 2:9)

SEED OF GRACE

When was the last time you closed your eyes to taste a delicious bite?
Do you enjoy your food or rush through meals?
Do you savor the flavor or eat on the run?
Today, for at least one meal, sit quietly and relish
the bounty God has given you.

Continue Your Journey

Blessed are the meek, for they will inherit the land.
Matthew 5:5

As summer softens into autumn
relax on the grassy hillside with Our Lord's disciples,
listening to Him along with the multitudes
and reflecting on God's lavish use of color
in His terrestrial cathedral
Earth

Autumn Hope
Enjoying Colors in God's Garden

Aah, autumn's glorious kaleidoscope of colors!

Don't clear away those remnants of summer blossoms too soon
    for the butterfly alights
        who notices not their gangly-ness
            but knows there is still juice to extract.

Find your garden. Make space and time to connect with God.

Nature always wears the colors of the spirit.
–Ralph Waldo Emerson[1]

AUTUMN HOPE

The color palette of autumn is striking.

I find myself wondering if this season is not more vibrant than spring.
I could not imagine thinking this a few weeks ago as the
last flowers of summer began fading.
I was sad to see all my inspiration go.
And then...came the Fall colors!

Leaves, mums, pumpkins, and shrubs
display a spectrum from bright yellow, orange, and red
through shades of pinks and lavenders
culminating in purples and burgundies.
Butterflies and bees still enjoy these hues along with humanity.

There is hope in these elements of the season.
There is new exquisiteness to be experienced.
It reminds me that the
autumn of my life can take on fresh color.

*I am confident of this, that the one who began a good work in
you will continue to complete it until the day of Christ Jesus.*
Philippians 1:6

REFLECT

Autumn introduces an abundance of multicolored leaves and berries for the birds, exhibiting bright fall colors — reds, purples, yellows — before the winter snows begin to fly. I marvel at how God created all of Nature around me — working in perfect harmony.

SEED OF GRACE

Joy brings color to our lives! In this season of exquisite complexion, it is a good time to discern what prevents you from feeling joyful. Daydream about how your life can enjoy new hues by easing up and slowing down. This doesn't happen on its own — it must be cultivated and nurtured — by you.
What "seeds of hope" will you plant today?

SEPTEMBER LESSONS

I thought the colors of my garden were nearly gone, but as I sit in September's sun
pleasant and warm
I glance up from my book to notice the dusty-lavender phlox
the
T
A
L
L
variety
undulating in pleasantly cool September air.

Lesson #1 — Water until your garden says it's enough.

Adjacent to me and the phlox, reddening foliage of buttercups long gone,
complement a newly planted bronze mum.

Lesson #2 — Do not remove spent stalks of no-longer-blossoming flora.

Hovering above, still clinging to her trellis, the clematis displays her leaves' new colors
— mottled light green and yellow — and her flowers' spidery centers
bereft of previous purple petals — light wispiness.

Lesson #3 — Beauty changes from season to season.

A red-hued rose still graces the area with lovely blossoms and buds,
enhanced by surrounding deep green perennial foliage.
Yon is the yellowish, creamy, peach-colored miniature rose —
adorning my gold and bronze statue of Madonna and Child.

Lesson #4 — Soft September shades abound.

Prolific marigolds — intense yellow and orange — line the driveway,
along with spiky green remnants of spring's irises.

Lesson #5 — When lifeless flowers fall, they leave us with landscape, still.

And there is more: variegated coleus, purple asters, white-tipped magenta petunias, which rebloomed, slimly escaping the yard waste bin.

The ultimate lesson from the garden and God
P A T I E N C E.

Adopt the pace of nature: her secret is patience.
–Ralph Waldo Emerson[2]

REFLECT

The garden helps me traverse the seasons of my life,
encouraging me to stay the course,
with patience and tenacity, realizing
there is goodness and beauty at all times.

SEED OF GRACE

Decide where and with whom you need patience.
Just for today.
Take one moment at a time,
So life does not overwhelm
And hope is certain.

CEDARS OF LEBANON

The cedar is a symbol of holiness, eternity, and peace.

I strolled along the rows and rows of potted shrubs.
The attendant asked, "Are you the plant whisperer?"
Did he sense something?
A calmness among the stretch of saplings?
A connection to God's creation?
(I hope so.)

I chose two tiny giant cedars
not knowing where I would plant them in my small
yard already brimming with trees and shrubs.
But they were small — then.

Cedars are giants.
What was I thinking?
Was I only looking at the special price?
(Perhaps the cedars were whispering to me.)

Now I sit between them, on my swing.
They have grown and
I realize they will soon outgrow this space.
Their graceful arms flutter in the autumn breeze.
(Is there really a breeze or are they just dancing with delight?)

Although I sit alone,
there is company here.
They offer silent companionship
A peaceful presence...

I feel as if I'm on a mountain — silent, immortal, resilient.
I feel as if I can do all that I must do today.
Tucked in between them
I am one with them, as in a forest,
and I feel their strength.

I must go inside now.
My work calls me.
I would rather stay here with my evergreens
in this place of everlastingness
this place of peace and eternity
this place of strength and calm.

*The trees of the Lord drink their fill,
the cedars of Lebanon,
which you planted.*

Psalm 104:16

REFLECT

Amid the quiet strength of trees, I am able to clear my mind of clutter,
frustration, disappointment, negative thoughts, and restlessness.
With prayer in my heart, inner peace and calmness lift my
spirits, And I can enjoy the "here and now moment"
with God by my side.

SEED OF GRACE

Jesus was a carpenter, a strong craftsman.
It is said that He had a mysterious fragrance about Him —
that of a cedar of Lebanon, the wood of His profession
and the tree from which he would one day hang.
Contemplate this as you sit near a tree.

RASPBERRY ROSE

The color and scent

    suggest its name.

I stoop to sniff,

    affirm the claim.

In raspberry scent

    it has no shame,

For beauty and grace

    my eyes do frame.

Not berry, but rose

    no one to blame,

For a rose is a rose

    by any other name.

Its beauty and grace

    from whence did came?

Not berry, but rose

    its claim to fame.

*What's in a name? That which we call a rose
by any other name would smell as sweet.*
–William Shakespeare, *Romeo and Juliet*[3]

Autumn Hope

REFLECT

A rose that smells like a raspberry?
God combines many things for my pleasure,
Today, I resolve to notice and appreciate His graceful gifts.
Where can I stop to smell some roses?

SEED OF GRACE

In order to "stop and smell the roses," one must first stop,
then bend forward, then breathe.
What rose, person, or circumstance will you examine today?
Make the commitment to pay attention,
and be inspired.

SILENT COMPANION

She sits
Still
On the garden chair opposite me.

I sit
Still
And marvel at her delicacy.

No book or pen
No conversation
She teaches me serenity

this tiny golden butterfly.
A skein of geese in the sky
has not more artistry than she.

Balmy breeze — lofty limbs asway
Stillness. Tranquility. She stays.
How can I leave?

I learn the essence of silent companionship
from this tiny golden butterfly.

You don't have to open your mouth to pray.
–Matthew Kelly[4]

Just open your heart.
–Cecile Smith[5]

REFLECT

When I reflect upon a butterfly circling around me, I must be very still so it will not flutter away. This helps me understand stillness — the stillness I must develop in order to listen and hear God speaking to me. When the butterfly alights, and I remain motionless, contemplating its loveliness, I feel the silence inside me where God's voice is heard. He whispers. I resolve to be silent to hear Him.

SEED OF GRACE

God sends His love through brief encounters with His creatures. Today, try to recognize His gifts which they bring. When you go to your garden spot to say prayers and have morning coffee, be inspired to enjoy the stillness of companionship with God!

THE SPARROW'S PRAYER

The sparrow calls me to the open window
her chirping is frenzied
I do not understand her plaintiff song
I go closer to see.

Is she summoning friends?
Is she warning of a close-by threat?
Is she lost and calling for help?

I listen, but
cannot decipher her message.
After all, she doesn't speak my language.

God's language is different too.
He speaks to my heart and my mind and my conscience
Sometimes in thoughts
Sometimes in words
Sometimes in feelings.
Sometimes directly to me and sometimes through others.

Often, I don't know exactly what He is asking of me.
So, as with the sparrow,
I must get closer to Him
to understand His message.

So do not be afraid; you are worth more than many sparrows.
Matthew 10:31

REFLECT

When I pray today, I will consider the faces of souls I may never meet —
those in trouble, those in need of help, those who need a friend.
God speaks to all people through His creation,
so, I will pray that they may hear the love and find the peace
He expresses in the sights and sounds of Nature.

SEED OF GRACE

Consider that God speaks in subtle ways, and sometimes you might not
recognize His voice. Ponder the ways He might speak to you today.
Learn to listen more carefully, because He is always calling you,
and He has a special mission for you.

SPIRITUAL BLANKETS

Today, the temperatures are again in the high 60s,
just like yesterday.
Due to an overcast sky, however,
I don't feel the same.
Yesterday, I was cozy and comfortable.
Today, it is not as pleasant to pray in the garden,
so, I don a sweater for warmth.

This is how it is with my prayers, as well.
On sunny days, I feel in touch with God.
I can feel Him in the warmth of the sun.
He caresses me with His balmy breezes, and
I have no doubt that He is here with me.

On not-so-sunny days, my thoughts are vague and
my prayers are overcast — distracted by
some looming episode or the busyness of
people, plans, and schedules.
Clouds hang over my homage, casting shadows.
Inspiration trembles in the chilliness.
My connection falters.

It is at times like this that I must look to another devotion to warm my thoughts.
I must seek more grace to envelop me, so I can feel His warmth.
Attend Mass.
Pray a rosary.
Adore Him.
Read Scripture.
Light a candle.
These established traditions are like a comfy blanket around my shoulders,
and I am reminded of the burden He carried on His own shoulders for me.
Once again, I am reconnected and feel His unfailing presence.

Rejoice in hope, endure in affliction, persevere in prayer.
Romans 12:12

Autumn Hope

REFLECT

I will ponder my favorite devotion and how I feel spiritually
when I revisit it. What connection to God does it give me?
Does our friendship deepen?

SEED OF GRACE

Envision prayer as a spiritual blanket.
Light a candle, attend Bible study, or sit in Nature.
Sense this familiar sacred warmth draped across your shoulders.

GRATITUDE

I would like to traverse through my day
      the way the hawk glides gracefully across the sky
                                   above
                                   the trees
     distant from the
          c
           a
         c
          o
           p
           h
          o
           n
            y
                    below

His path is unlike the straight, rigid path of the airplane or
      the
  fl   t t   i n g
    u t   e r   -by
  of the monarch or
the quick close-to-the-ground
                  d
                    a
                     r
                      t
                       i
                        n
                         g
                            of the sparrow...

Autumn Hope

I wonder if
      looking down upon me
            so seemingly carefree
                  swaying in my swing
the hawk wonders what it's like to be me

I look carefree to him
              He looks free of care to me
                          Would we want to trade places?

Gratitude turns what we have into enough.
        –Aesop[6]

REFLECT

Often, I am guilty of desiring someone else's "greener grass."
I call it hope to mask my envy.
When I contemplate the unique person that God made me,
with my talents, strengths, sensitivities, and weaknesses,
I realize how precious I am to Him.
Today, I choose to focus on what I have and use it to give glory to God.

SEED OF GRACE

Think of someone who seems to have it better than you.
Imagine switching places and consider what you would give up —
all those blessings God provides graciously, specifically to you.
All that richness — sacrificed for some elusive longing.

AUTUMN SPECTACULAR

I could look at my chrysanthemums all day long — forever.
A circular arrangement spills up over my low brick wall.

Oh, so many yellows! Lemon, gold, amber, and ochre,
each uniquely vibrant.

Lilac! Magenta! and every hue in between — pink tinge, blushing burgundy,
ruddy rosiness — blessing all beholders.

Then there are the tiny white button-shaped blossoms
that change to a rosy red from their edges inward, as they age,
gently obliterating all white.

Other plants that have ceased to bloom, lend a backdrop of mellowed greens for
these soft but brilliant colors of autumn;
and standing sentinel over them all is this season's last miniature red rose.
The sun spills splendidly across my yard and beyond,
enhancing the contrast between fire bush and majestic blue spruce.
Shadows and patches of light flicker on distant grass
as the breeze plays gently with branches.
Wispy clouds sail in a blue sky.
Pure red impatiens lend an impressive display
neath my old dilapidated bench…

This vibrant vista creates a heavenly panorama.

Eyes close,

face lifts to an autumn sun,

hair gives way to gentle breezes,

Heaven surrounds and

imagination wanders.

Is this like Heaven?

Gazing at God forever?

Being in His Presence?

Or is this just earthly pleasure?

Eye has not seen, ear has not heard, nor has it so much as dawned on man what God has prepared for those who love him.
1 Corinthians 2:9

REFLECT

During these coming seasons, I resolve to get out into Nature
more often — connect with God through fall and
winter walks and talks.

SEED OF GRACE

Creation is but a faint suggestion of God's mastery,
and yet delights our eye, our heart, our mind, our soul.
God gifted you with this splendor here on Earth;
imagine what He has planned in His Celestial Paradise for you!
How much greater the awe when you finally look directly upon His face!
Find a place to connect to extraordinary Nature surrounding you.

SHINING THROUGH

One of the most invigorating sights in my garden
is the sun shining through a petal or leaf.

The brilliant translucence of color is unimaginable:
green becomes yellow,
red is softened and
ivory becomes white,
even dark purple shines brilliantly orange.

I could perhaps imagine myself this way:
Politeness could become caring;
consideration — kindness;
accommodation — hospitality;
if I let the Son shine through me.

All I have to do is turn my face toward Him and accept the warming of His grace.
If a cloud enters, I stay the course, for it will pass,
and once again, His brilliance will shine through me.

He was transfigured before them;
his face shone like the sun and his clothes became white as light.
Matthew 17:2

Autumn Hope

REFLECT

This autumn,
I will choose an evening when the sun is shining through,
step outside, and turn my face to its rays,
feeling God's warmth shine through my heart.

SEED OF GRACE

Autumn's evening sun reflects through the changing leaves,
creating the myriad colors that cannot be described.
Today, let Jesus, the Son of God, shine through you
creating colors of caring, tints of kindness, hues of hospitality,
the glow of goodness, and the look of luminous love.
Welcome the Holy Spirit into your day!

PERSPECTIVE

One branch of my lovely pine tree hangs much lower than the others.

The tree is large and arches over the driveway, so it must be trimmed every year to allow for the car to pass beneath. The trimming procedure is quite a delicate undertaking, since I have inherited "over-pruning syndrome" from my grandfather, whose origins harken from a small Italian hillside village. I don't know if this character trait is peculiar to Italians, or just my Nonno, but even so, I have it.

Once the clippers are in action, they take command. So, after several branches fall, I have learned to step back to get the big picture, circling round and round to assess my artistry from different perspectives. When everything else is shapely, I check the lone limb again and again. From one vantage point, it continually looks out of harmony — needing to be discarded — and yet, from another angle, it is perfectly positioned.

This inspires me to consider perspective in a philosophical way — looking at the same thing from different directions, various backgrounds, multiple histories and experiences. The world is filled with people from different families, neighborhoods, and communities, each with their own variegated perception, and I must acknowledge the validity of their views.

This low pine branch remains today. It belongs there. I notice it every time I pull into my driveway, reminding me about perception and how others may see things differently than I. It's a good perspective to keep in mind.

Peace cannot be kept by force. It can only be achieved by understanding.
–Albert Einstein[7]

REFLECT

As I advance in age and wisdom,
I am more apt to accept different points of view.
Knowing why others think the way they do heightens my
understanding, while also helping me learn to care about them.

Look up!
Three decades ago, when my children were young, we would lie in the grass under a tree and look up.
I could not believe how that view changed the perspective of the tree and the mindset of our life.

SEED OF GRACE

Upon hearing another's opinion, allow for their different point of view,
and ask God to give you the grace to really listen and consider it.
In this way, your own insight will broaden,
and your life will increase with more meaningful interrelationships,
which is the beginning of the understanding of peace.

ETERNAL LIFE

Sedum is in full bloom.
Butterflies and bees crowd on each blossom to sip its sweet nectar.
They are unaware of each other until they bump another and
quickly flit to an uninhabited space.

Their focus is the nectar: God's sweet juice.

These airborne insects seem to know this is one of the last sources of the season.
Their frantic activity conveys an urgency to drink as much as possible,
as if their life depended on it — almost as if it would help them "Live Forever,"
as the common name of this plant suggests.
The truth is: They won't survive the coming winter.

I, however, have access to God's sweet graces in all Seasons,
just for the asking.
And if I 'drink enough' it will bring me Eternal Life.
Perhaps, I should adopt the urgent frenzy of the butterfly and bee.

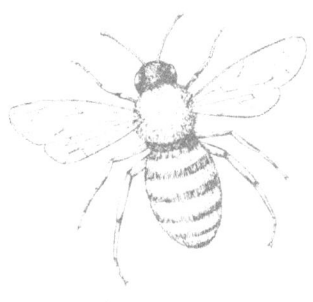

Whoever eats my flesh and drinks my blood has eternal life,
and I will raise him on the last day.
John 6:54

Autumn Hope

REFLECT

As we get older,
we contemplate hope of eternal life with God and
vow to embrace the graces He gives us, to use them wisely.
I do not want to waste a moment selfishly or needlessly,
but follow the path God has prepared for me leading to Eternity.

SEED OF GRACE

Think of an occasion when you let an opportunity for receiving
grace pass you by. Then ask Jesus in the Blessed Sacrament to make
you aware of future grace-filled moments. Be specific. Look ahead.
Ask for the grace you will need today.

WHY THE SKY

While saying the "Angelus" prayer
looking up at the sky,
I felt God's presence.
Why the sky?

It is here, but out of my reach.
It is constant, but ever-changing.
It is untouchable, and yet surrounds my world.

It sends good things for me to treasure —
Sunshine, warmth, rain, snow;
refreshment, breezes, and joy;
rainbows for childlike wonder.

It's immense
It's indescribable
It has power over me
It sends me light and dark,
day for work and night for rest

Oh, envy, as I watch the birds soar in it,
closer to God than I.

I am here with you every day beneath my endless sky. Just look up.

Later, the same day —
I found a scribble on a scrap of napkin:
"Serve God in love, like a Father, not a Master,
with a super abundance of goodness to all."

Immediately, the feeling I had earlier —
while looking at the sky, feeling God close by — returned.
I felt His loving care for me;
that He was interested and involved in my goings and comings;
smiling down on me in love.
I did not feel a Master at all, even though He is:
a Loving Master.

See what love the Father has bestowed on us that we may be called the children of God.
1 John 3:1

Autumn Hope

REFLECT

Father, help me follow your example to nurture
the children in my life as You care for me:
with loving attentiveness, refreshment, and childlike wonder.
In this way, my loved ones may inspire families the world over,
all of us under the same immense sky!

SEED OF GRACE

Ponder the image of Jesus slowly ascending into Heaven,
His hands extended out.
While His disciples gaze upward with wonder and awe,
He speaks these loving words,
"I am with you always, until the end of the age." (Matthew 28:20)
Find comfort when you look up at the sky.

NEW AWAKENINGS

I open my eyes to the
rooftop,
slopes,
chimney,
intersecting angles,

blue sky and
sunshine swelling,
shadowy patterns changing,
perching and
chirping.

God's Creation and
man's creation in
delightful harmony.
The sight is
awakening.

No need for the
mechanical rooster.
How can I sleep
with this astonishment
awaiting?!

Here he stands…gazing through the windows…
"Arise, my beloved, my beautiful one, and come!"
Song of Songs 2:9-10

REFLECT

Morning is like a new promise from God.
Another opportunity to receive and give:
receive my new mission through which I can inspire others;
give myself a chance to hear God's voice in everyday moments —
like each day's dawning.
I will decide what I will receive and give today.

SEED OF GRACE

Describe your morning routine.
Can you approach morning with such wonder instead
of in a fog, fumbling around for coffee?
Ask God to tell you how.
Then listen for His advice.

CHRYSANTHEMUMS AND PUMPKINS

I would never put their colors together in a fashion sort of way.

But here, in Nature — God's Garden — they complement each other perfectly.

In my limited perception,

    I cannot wear pink with orange,

        but God created a multitude of colors,

            even those I cannot see.

He created them in a variance of hues,

    yet, I may consider pumpkins just "orange"

        and chrysanthemums simply "pink."

I know a young lady who, while in a coma, glimpsed Heaven.

She tried to describe it, but all she could exclaim was,

    "Oh! The colors! The colors of Heaven!"

And so, I gaze upon Heaven's hues to renew my spirit and calm my heart,

    knowing that God is here.

Mordecai left the king's presence clothed in a
royal robe of violet and of white cotton,
with a large crown of gold and a
mantle of fine crimson linen.
Esther 8:15

REFLECT

When I observe Nature in this season of change, with its prolific array of colors, I imagine that God might be trying to tell me to notice the appealing colors of the people around me.

SEED OF GRACE

What new colors will you challenge yourself to see today?
Gazing upon them, which ones renew your spirit and calm your heart?
Do they help you connect with God?

WONDERFUL FAULTS

The bright yellow leaves lay where they have fallen
atop the shadow of my barren mulberry tree.

If I look at the shadow, I see only an ominous outline.
If I focus on the leaves, I see only their pattern on the ground.
But when I gaze across both together, beyond the details,
their designs intermingle and present an extraordinary phenomenon.

People are like this — full of beauty and faults.
Our faults cause us to struggle, and our struggles make us better.
So, without faults, we could not improve. It is a wise plan.
And I must earnestly endeavor to
seek and enjoy the wonder of all people.

I must remember to gaze past perceived faulty details of
family and friends, children and adults,
to discover the entire unique creature in all its splendor,
designed by God in His image —
to be wonderful!

*For we are his handiwork,
created in Christ Jesus for the good works
that God has prepared in advance,
that we should live in them.*
Ephesians 2:10

REFLECT

How can I react differently today?
Ask.
Then listen.

SEED OF GRACE

Think of connections in your upcoming day where you can look for the promise in the people of your life. Plan ahead. Intend to appreciate each person who comes your way. Pause before you react, and look past the ominous shadow of their faults. Remember, they also struggle to improve.

NOVEMBER SKY

Clear. Crisp. Clean.

Wispy white clouds traveling swiftly, gently.

Bright sun

refreshing my soul,

inspiring homage to the Almighty who sends me these gifts.

A craggy canopy of beautifully bared branches

silhouette across a clear blue and white skyscape.

Limbs — bare and brave — with seed pods at the top

seem to soar off into the wide blue wonder called "sky."

Looking up, I see endless deep blue

reaching infinitely to the heavens

suggesting such a magnificent journey.

The month of Thanksgiving

full of feast and family.

I will not forget the November sky when giving thanks.

*The beauty of the celestial height and the pure firmament,
heaven itself manifests its glory.*
Sirach 43:1

REFLECT

Do I see God in the trees' bare limbs — as beautiful pieces
of Nature's perfect organic puzzle, rather than a depressing sign?
What other phases of this season have their unique changing beauty?
How do they simply, superbly, and mysteriously reflect the divine?

SEED OF GRACE

Take nothing for granted, even your responsibilities,
for all are gifts from above, which He planned for you long ago.
Today, notice all things, big and small, and realize a blessing in each.

Journey through Transition

You fixed all the limits of the earth; summer and winter you made.
Psalm 74:17

Discover God in the silent intricacies of winter —
steep, rugged canopies of leafless trees
sun's rays flickering through onto forest floor and bare lawns
silent stirrings of majestic evergreens
snowfall
hushed white-scapes
pale sky.

Winter Wonder
Staying Connected in God's Garden

"Listen to the silence!"

A winter storm had fallen upon the city while I was at midnight Mass with two of my sons. Driving home was very stressful for me. Roads hadn't been cleared yet and traffic was unexpectedly busy. When I finally arrived in the safety of my driveway, all I wanted to do was get inside. Safe and warm.

My sons were oblivious to my anxiety and the reason for it. They were probably marveling at the snow-covered world, and thinking of snowballs and sleds on the morrow. A White Christmas!

As I fumbled with the key and prepared to step inside, my son paused — looking out upon a serene world, he said,
"Wait! Listen to the silence."
I was in no mood for pausing or silence — only warmth and rest.
So, I regret to say, I stepped inside and lost that moment, forever.

Whether you live in snow-laden places or not,
don't lose those precious winter moments:
A special silence permeates the season of winter.

*What good is the warmth of summer,
without the cold of winter
to give it sweetness?*
—John Steinbeck[1]

TRANSITIONS

Winter came in a day
Crisp November sky
gave way to an alabaster December landscape
during the night
white sky, white land, white trees, white garden.

Stark, cold, windy.
Transitions.
New seasons. New Interests.
New habits, sleeping patterns, eating schedules
Revive, rejuvenate, and remake.

Embrace it.
Accept the cold, white, windy new world.
Renew *your* world.
Your life.

Renew
Isn't this what Advent is all about?
A new chance. A new outlook. A new perspective.
A savior.

Advent
A season to replenish my soul.
God restores my world
Away with the old garden to prepare the new.

The Lord is my shepherd; I shall not want. In verdant pastures he gives me repose;
Beside restful waters he leads me; he refreshes my soul.
He guides me in right paths for his name's sake.
Even though I walk in the dark valley I fear no evil;
for you are at my side with your rod and your staff that give me courage.

Psalm 23:1-4

REFLECT

How do I start? Where do I begin?
I will list three ways I can reconnect with someone.
I will pray for them at the window for a week
as I gaze at the slumbering landscape.
Then I will enact my plan
and begin.

SEED OF GRACE

Winter is a perfect season to begin again!
Reconnect with friends and family
Ask forgiveness for wrongs committed
Regenerate relationships
Contemplate wonders and miracles in the silence

'TWAS A MONTH BEFORE CHRISTMAS

It came just in time.
Just when I was beginning to stress amidst the chaos.
Just when I was frantic about finishing the preparations for His coming.
How can I do it all?
The cards, the greetings, the presents, the wrapping, the mailing, the choosing, the buying.
The food, the meals, the grocery shopping, the preparations, the cleanup, again and again.
The cookies, the candies, the baking, and the making.
How do I simplify?

I pause and think of the Holy Family in this season,
for they, themselves, endured a stressful time
trying to arrive at a place of rest.
Me too, I think.
But I must continue.
Joseph and I have no choice.

When the hour is come, at last,
Joseph and Mary and their new baby, Jesus, relax and enjoy each other.
A Holy Family together.
This is my purpose.
This is my goal and, though tired and weary, the time will come to relax and enjoy my family.
A holy end to my frantic search for calm family joy.

The cards, the food, the gifts.
They all make sense now.
These are simply my imperfect attempts to follow the Holy Family
in search of sacred togetherness.
Next Advent, I must remember where my journey will lead me.
Then, I will embrace the busyness, remembering that
I am on the road to Bethlehem with Jesus, Mary, and Joseph!

They went in haste and found Mary and Joseph,
and the baby lying in the manger…
Luke 2:16

REFLECT

Introspection helps make sense of the busyness of the season
and the importance of focusing on one thing at a time.

SEED OF GRACE

You need not worry that you might waste time doing
something frivolous in your hurriedness,
for every preparation carries its own importance.
A simple life doesn't mean that you don't have a lot to do.
Rather, you do one thing at a time, giving each the attention it deserves.

WINTER'S WONDERS

I relax in my hammock on this wintry day — chilly and clear.
It's too cold to be out here, but I am bundled up.
The sun summoned me — so I came.
It shines on my hammock and me, warming us both,
and I realize it is much earlier in the day than usual.

In autumn, I waited for afternoon to capture a sliver of sun
in between shade trees here on my hammock.
Now, I look up toward warming rays shining through branches with no leaves.
Isn't it amazing that God planned such splendor for us?
Even in the losing of leaves and the baring of branches
I am now blessed with long afternoons of winter warmth —
shorter days, yet longer sun.

Winter
often a time of despair
seen as the time of Nature's demise.
But my hammock view would suggest otherwise:

Pale blue sky, hazy gray clouds, sun's warming rays, and pulsating pines.
Shapes of deciduous limbs — artistry against the sky — strong and delicate.
Leftover leaves cover, as a carpet, the languishing lawn.
Berries cling to shrubs for hungry birds.
Air, firm and fresh.
I'm not cold anymore.

Thank you, God, for these invigorating changes — this winter bounty!

*God looked at everything he had made, and he found it very good.
Evening came, and morning followed…*
Genesis 1:31

Winter Wonder

REFLECT

I have heard dead trees in the winter referred to as "ugly."
But to me, their barren limbs are beautiful!
Where else could I be missing the wonders of winter sent by God?

SEED OF GRACE

Many people bemoan winter. Cold. Snow. Ice. Rain.
Yet, God sends it just like spring, summer, and autumn.
Take a closer look at His gifts and winter blessings.
Then, thank Him, and find a way to enjoy them.

MADONNA

Mary, the Mother of the season
Mary, the Mother of the event
Mary, the Mother of God

The Canticle of Mary

And Mary said:
"My soul proclaims the greatness of the Lord;
my spirit rejoices in God my savior.
For he has looked upon his handmaid's lowliness;
behold, from now on will all ages call me blessed.
The Mighty One has done great things for me,
and holy is his name.
His mercy is from age to age
to those who fear him.
He has shown might with his arm,
dispersed the arrogant of mind and heart.
He has thrown down the rulers from their thrones
but lifted up the lowly.
The hungry he has filled with good things;
the rich he has sent away empty.
He has helped Israel his servant,
remembering his mercy,
according to his promise to our fathers,
to Abraham and to his descendants forever."

Luke 1:46-55

Mary treasured all these things and reflected on them in her heart.
Luke 2:19

REFLECT

Like the Mother of God,
I treasure this season of the Incarnation of Jesus —
"the wonderment of Nature!"
I reflect joyfully on these events in my heart and,
like Mary, I will proclaim His mercy, might, and magnificence.

SEED OF GRACE

Our Blessed Mother, referred to as "the woman wrapped in silence,"
knows when to speak —
praising God's greatness, His might, His holiness, His mercy,
and His promise. Mary is a good friend to listen to.

THE NATIVITY

A grace of this mystery is detachment from worldly goods —
the Holy Family spending the birth of God's only-begotten Son
in abject poverty in the piercing cold —
food brought to them by poor shepherds willing to share what little they had.
Why? Because there was something more important happening here,
which made material goods insignificant.

Thankfully, there are God-given blessings of this world —
like this evening's winter sunset that transformed before my very eyes,
taking my breath away at every seamless metamorphosis,
leaving no words to aptly describe the horizon.
Is this to be considered a worldly good?

Discernment, then, is the virtue I need to cultivate:
From what on this earth should I detach myself,
and to what should I turn my attention?
This feat cannot be accomplished with a single thought,
nor in a moment;
but with a new year ahead of me,
I can make great progress throughout the coming days.

At this time of ushering in a new year,
some may call this prioritizing or
focusing on seemingly significant things of life.
I prefer to take the opposite approach —
weed out the superfluous,
leaving only meaningful matters to put in order.

The winter sunset inspires me to attach myself to components of vitality,
like the Star of Bethlehem astonished the shepherds with the magnitude of the moment.

*The angel said to them…"In a manger You will find an infant wrapped
in swaddling clothes." The shepherds said to one another: "Let us go over
to Bethlehem and see this event which the Lord has made known to us."*
Luke 2:12, 15

Winter Wonder

REFLECT

What makes my life meaningful?
How can I achieve serenity?
Moving forward, I must first look deeply inward.
Thoughtful introspection is necessary for my life to grow.

SEED OF GRACE

Every moment of your life, you have a choice
between something insignificant
or a God-given blessing.
You may need some help recognizing the difference.
So, ask.
"Lord, help me choose wisely."

JOY TO THE WORLD

From its recent splendor, my discarded Christmas tree now lies on the brush pile awaiting its final demise. It brought many hours of pleasure and delight as family gathered 'round and nearby. The tree's twinkling presence and splendor became a sparkling backdrop for future memories. We remember it fondly.

Every Christmas tree begins with its own unique attributes — size, shape, fullness, type of needles. Yet, even the scraggly "Charlie Brown" variety, with just the right amount of attention, can inspire joy. I too have my own unique talents to offer the world, to accomplish wonderful things. With ornaments of love and nurturing tinsel, I can leave behind not just a legacy of good deeds but also warm memories of kindness.

Will I remember this Spirit of Christmas that filled my heart and home? Can I treat others with the same love I felt in the glow of the twinkling lights? Will I give my gifts graciously to family and neighbors?

I used to scoff at Christmas-in-July marketing, but the beauty and glow of the Christmas tree with all its blessings should be present in my heart year-round. "Joy to the World" is not only a seasonal song I can sing in December, but a remembered melody to live by, radiating from the crevices of my heart.

The angel said to them, "Do not be afraid; for behold, I proclaim to you good news of great joy that will be for all the people…"
Luke 2:10

REFLECT

Aside from singing "Joy to the World" year-round,
there are many reminders I can insert into my days:
set up a cell phone notification;
place my tiny porcelain angel on my bathroom vanity;
frame my favorite Christmas card and hang it on my bedroom wall;
put something in my car where I will see it often.
Spread the joy!

SEED OF GRACE

Think of a remnant of this Christmas to keep on your desk
or kitchen counter or cell phone reminding you of the love
that was given to you on that first Christmas day, and encouraging
you daily to live always in the spirit of giving.

SUNRISE, SUNSET

Mornings are like the Nativity
Full of new hope and precious promise
Watch the new dawn in anticipation

Evenings are like the Ascension
Full of wonder and awe
Watch until gone
Await a new dawn

The Lord has turned all our sunsets into sunrise.
–Saint Clement[2]

Winter Wonder

REFLECT

What will I do with the grand rising of my new dawn?
How will I thank God for this gift of painted horizons that bookend my days?
When evening comes, will I have filled this day with wonder and awe?

SEED OF GRACE

"Await a new dawn"
is a lovely reciprocal sentiment, almost guaranteeing the next day;
while at the same time, decreasing the urgency of this day.
Be thoughtful to celebrate the day's end before
hoping for the new dawn.

SUNSHINE AND MY NEW FRONT DOOR

Our house had been broken into and the door ruined, so we had to replace it. Now, every morning I am greeted by prismed sunshine streaming through the stained-glass window, as I descend the stairs into my day.

We never would have changed that old door if the other hadn't been destroyed. Thankfully, God knows my love of sunshine, so He chose this blessing for me. This attractive door even brings joy to my neighbors, who notice it as they drive by and speak of its lovely design. God always brings good out of evil — a blessing out of a misfortune.

I opened the door to a glorious "spring morning!" on January 9. The Baptism of the Lord! I lingered, marveling at Nature and breathing in the goodness of God's world. The skies were open, the sun shone, and I could almost hear His voice:

"You are my beloved daughter. On you My favor rests."

The next moment, I opened the back door to put out trash. The sun had not yet made its way around there, and it felt cold and foreboding. The difference was startling. I put the trash out quickly, closing the door. I did not want to linger and breathe there, for it was not inviting and I had no desire to enter that world.

I thought about my life with God's warmth and love and light in contrast to what it would be like without Him. I thought about how He orchestrated the replacement of my front door so He could greet me every morning, even when I forget to say "Hello" to Him. I yearned for more closeness with Him, and found myself on the front stoop donning my jacket and hat, drinking in the warmth of God's love on a chilly January morning. He is always here for me — I just need to notice Him.

I am the light of the world.
Whoever follows me will not walk in darkness, but will have the light of life.
John 8:12

REFLECT

Jesus knocks on the door of my heart.
If I open it, He will say, "Come sit with Me for a while."
I need to make time for Him each day to get to know Him,
and myself better.

SEED OF GRACE

Identify ways in which God orchestrated change in your life.
Reflect on them for a few moments and give thanks for His thoughtfulness.
Ask Him to help you notice Him each day.
He is waiting to greet you.

LIVING WATER

The snow covers the garden.
The fence. The trees. The garden bench.
Cold and stark.
How do I see God here?

Maybe He is beneath, in the seeds, which will flourish in spring.
Of course. But there is more.
He is here now.
Perhaps the cold and starkness come from me.

When I neglect to open my heart to let Him in
He does not leave.
He waits. Out in the cold.
I resist. Too busy?

The wind howls like my life without Him.
The goodness is there.
I see it, but
I don't recognize Him.

Until
Finally
I bring Him inside and,
He becomes Living Water.

Whoever believes in me…'Rivers of living water will flow from within him.'
John 7:38

Winter Wonder

REFLECT

Rivers of living water flowing from within me!
And all I have to do is believe in Him.
What a promise!

SEED OF GRACE

When you think of something as tangible as melting snow,
you can sense the essence of God's Nature.

WINTER'S TREES

I love the trees
that in winter keep hold of their brownish leaves.
I never saw this. How?
I look more carefully now.

I don't know their names
only common ones can I acclaim
(although no tree is common)
whose leaves fall
to identify them all.

They look quite sterile
The naked trees without apparel
while these others seem to fly
texture against the sky.

What a lovely
discovery
on this gray
desolate day.

Let us not get so busy or live so fast that we can't listen to the music of the meadow or the symphony that glorifies the forest.
–Dale Carnegie[3]

REFLECT

I am surprised that I never noticed these winter trees that retain an element of earlier seasons. Was I indifferent? Too busy or distracted? Did I forget to look up or connect with natural beauty around me? In order to observe the wonder, one must pause, creating time to be still and see.

SEED OF GRACE

Identify natural beauty that is within your line of vision.
Do you notice it often or miss it in the hubbub of your day?
Look through windows at trees or walk among them.
Don't forget to look up!

HIDDEN PRESENCE

The snow brightens the earth.

    Even at night, I can see better outside.

        The landscape becomes more clear.

            Objects I could not see in the shadows

                Take on a definitive shape — white but distinguishable.

                    Although hidden 'neath the glistening carpet,

                I know where everything lies.

So it is with the Holy Eucharist

    I come to His Presence.

        He is hidden in the white Host.

            And yet, I can see things better when I am with Him.

                The shadows of doubt and indecision disappear

                    Allowing me to see more clearly.

*Never give up this daily intimate contact with
Jesus as the real living person — not just the idea.*
–Saint Teresa of Calcutta[4]

Winter Wonder

REFLECT

Doubts cloud my vision, and indecision interferes.
I ponder for a moment an aspect of Nature,
then realize I don't need everything spelled out.
I turn my difficulties over to Jesus
and calm clarity materializes.

SEED OF GRACE

Where will you connect with Jesus today?
Consider the possibility of His Being present in your plant near the window.
Why not contemplate that for a moment?

HERE IN THE GRAY

Snow in the sky
Snow on the ground
Everywhere I look
Whiteness surrounds.

Some would say
"What a gray, gray day
I cannot wait
Till it all goes away."

I, on the other hand
See beauty that abounds
On this dark, gray day
Where whiteness astounds.

On trees and cars
And rooftops around,
Sidewalks and streets
Snow mounds are found.

Slush becomes ice
As temperatures go down
And care must be taken
When walking aground.

We hope for the sun
As we glimpse through our fear
But waiting is wasted
For the Son is always near.

He hides in the grayness
He smiles through the sun
No matter the weather
With us He is one.

Thus he makes the snow like wool, and spreads the frost like ash;
He disperses hail like crumbs. Who can withstand his cold?
Yet when again he issues his command, it melts them…
Psalm: 147:16-18

Winter Wonder

REFLECT

When God seems untouchable, invisible, beyond recognition,
I must stop and look for Him.
He is not hiding from me — He is always near.
His grace invites me to seek Him.

I wrote this poem while driving to work through slush-covered streets lined with plowed snow.
As words entered my mind, I pulled to the curb and jotted them down.
To wait would have meant lost inspiration.

SEED OF GRACE

Seize hold of inspiration when it comes your way.
Accept what you see and find the beauty.
God is in the here and now,
not the morrow that may never come.

THE SHAPE OF GOD

The snow clings to each branch, taking its shape.
So too must I grasp God's grace —
take on His shape —
becoming one.

With God as the snow and I the branch,
I let Him enfold me in His embrace
to receive His blessings.

What if I am the snow?
I must hold fast with every frozen droplet —
wrap myself around Him,
find unison with Him,
conform to His contour.

At times, He will come to me,
enriching me.
Other times, I must seek Him,
envelop Him.

Either way
I reap the benefits
as
I become like Him.

*And I tell you…seek and you will find…
the one who seeks, finds…*
Luke 11:9-10

REFLECT

The vision of being covered by God is very comforting —
a feeling of intimacy. Thinking about God in such
a personal way deepens my connection to Him.

SEED OF GRACE

How can you embrace God? Take His shape? What does this mean?
Be like Him? Do what He would do?

Today, resolve to embrace each situation,
trying to find a divine shape.

WHAT DO YOU SEEK?

If you want to know silence
There it is
   Through the glass
   In a snow-covered world
   Profuse and plush
   Mounded on the ground
   Lovely and lush.
   If you want to know stillness
There it is
   Lining limbs
   Cushioning chairs
   Following fence and
   Swallowing cares.
   If you want to know beauty
There it is
   Look about
   At low-lying branches
   Covered shrubs
   Hidden benches and
   Stone cherubs.
   If you want to know peace
There it is
   Flurries afloat
   Fires aflame
   The chill remote
   Delight just the same.
   If you still seek stillness
Here it is
   In a snow-laden world
   Covering our cares
   Veiling our doubts
   Inspiring our prayers
Through the glass.

*I love so much a soul's desire to receive Me,
that I hasten to it each time it summons Me by its yearnings.*

–Words of Jesus to Saint Margaret Mary Alacoque[5]

REFLECT

Winter brings a penetrating silence
and sometimes
I hear best in the deepest absence of sound.

SEED OF GRACE

What do you yearn for?
Contemplate the desires of your heart and
talk to Jesus about them in winter's stillness.
What do you hear Him say?

THE VIRTUE OF PREPARATION

Snow covers my springtime chair.

Inside, I wait
for melting
for sunshine
for a few more weeks
until I can sit "inside" my garden.
But Nature is not waiting.
It is preparing —
moistening the earth and roots for new growth.

New Growth.
Should I aspire to that?
Am I a seasonal creature
to be renewed each year?
How should I grow this season?
Perhaps I should be preparing instead of waiting.

Patience is said to be a virtue
but preparation transcends it.
Lent is preparation for spiritual growth —
the spring of my soul.

My garden teaches me why I must prepare:
spring is coming!

So too, you also must be prepared, for at an hour
you do not expect, the Son of Man will come.
Matthew 24:44

REFLECT

Preparing my heart for God is emulating the garden in winter —
each day a hope to "uncover" new life hidden within me.
This season is a time to rid my life of weeds and rocks,
and upturn the soil of my heart.
This season is the time to create space for growth —
preparing to be changed, nurtured, strengthened, understood, fertile —
to grow in faith, hope, and love.

SEED OF GRACE

How will you prepare for the Lord? How will you prepare
the soil of your soul for the seed of renewal to take root?
Allow Lent to cultivate this virtue of preparation.

BLESSINGS

On this unseasonably warm
February afternoon
in my backyard,
I sip my coffee and have a snack,
warming myself by the
small fire I just built.

Here,
I realize that the need to
eat, drink, and stay warm
are gifts from God
for me to enjoy.

I used to see them as
duties to be done,
even burdens to bear —
to prepare each meal,
to pay the heating bill.

Now,
I realize these are not chores
to fill the hours of my day
with the mundane.
These are blessings
to *fulfill* my days.

Forgive me, Lord,
for my weak vision and
lack of gratitude.
Help me to recognize and
appreciate your gifts
every day from now on.

Martha, Martha, you are anxious and worried about many things…
Luke 10:41

REFLECT

If I had been named Martha, scripture would be accurate,
for I have lived too much of my life anxiously — worrying
about children, money, and "getting it all done."

SEED OF GRACE

Consider *your* responsibilities of the coming day and
identify the blessings promised within each task.
Today, remember to look for the sacred in every activity.
Are you able to think of your basic needs as blessings sent by God?
Try to see them as opportunities to bask in His presence!

COFFEE & CREATION

Nature's chill
Gentle wind
My snuggly winter coat
A strip of sunlight
My garden chair
A cup of coffee.
What called me here?

Creation surrounds me —
Birds gently sing
Trees bud
Sprouts and shoots shout out spring
Clematis begins its climb
Daffodils send up buds.

I sit
I think of many things
Bygone and yet to come
But I cannot escape His
Sacred Presence here.

My sliver of sun has moved
My coffee is gone
I stay, my fingers stiff and red with cold.
What keeps me here?

He is here, amidst His creation
I praise Him with my pleasure
I praise Him here
Where He lives.

*Let us stand fast in what is right, and prepare our souls for trial.
Let us wait upon God's strengthening aid and say to him:
"O Lord, you have been our refuge in all generations."*
   –Saint Boniface[6]

Winter Wonder

REFLECT

What brings me to this place?
God's presence.
I will be still and listen for His voice,
contemplating His message to me,
and how it relates to my destiny.
What brings me to this place?

SEED OF GRACE

Where do you find Divine Presence?
Do you seek it?
When you find it, do you stay?
Today, take note of where you are and why you're there.
Consider what keeps you wherever you are.

Afterword

THE ETERNAL MOMENT

Cars and trucks speed past my stately redbud tree
so closely, its limbs respond in a whoosh, then recover, gently swaying.
Do the drivers notice the morning?
Beautiful wispy blue-white sky,
sun beaming on the street,
the redbud on the boulevard,
the world
and me?

God calls them lovingly but does not force.
He lives in each moment with us.

Can they see the urgency?
Will the sun shine on the morrow?
Will the redbud survive to the next season?
Will they even be speeding by
another day?

Time is not a curse to hurry us
but a blessing to make us notice,
to realize the moment of now
and capture it.
It is a one-time gift
this
eternal
moment.

End Note

How do I deserve this?
I have lots of things on my list for this day,
but my "work" place is here — in the garden — although it feels more like pleasure.
My garden is where I belong. How can I leave this place? How can I leave these gifts?
How can I leave *them* — Jesus and Mary, the saints, and angels?
They all surround me in glory in my garden.

I would love to connect with you!
Please send me an email with your thoughts and experiences.
I would enjoy speaking at your next event,
or leading a prayer group discussion,
or meeting you in your garden.
You may contact me at

CecileSmith.com

Thank you for reading my book.

Gratitude and Appreciation

I thank God for His friendship, for Nature, for the four seasons; for flowers and birds, trees and sky, sunshine and rain; for His words given to me through my pencil, and coming alive on my paper; and for the loveliest of friends and supporters who have helped bring this book to fruition. I offer my profound gratitude and appreciation to the following people who assisted, encouraged, and inspired me. They have become my kindred spirits.

My "Seeds of Grace": Chris Higgins, Colette Massey, Denise Harris, Pat Henderson, and Lucian Smith. Initially, Chris and Colette sat around the pool on summer days and read my first reflections. It was from their response that I knew I had to continue. Denise, Pat and Lucian joined in reading new pieces as I wrote them, sending their likes and dislikes, suggestions and affirmations for weeks upon weeks, which turned into months upon months of invaluable feedback. Without their support I would not have continued writing.

My "first readers": Diane McCullough, Sarah Beth Imperi, Maura Lein, Julie Barthel, Amy Hayes, Pat and Mary Ashcraft, Sherrin Kay Ashcraft, Diane Fetty, Leslie and Bella Smith, Julie Foley, Edith Bellisari, Anne Snyder, Denise Harris, Pat Henderson, and Lucian Smith who, when the time came, came through — reading the entire manuscript on a deadline, marking it with gentle corrections, assertions, and personal contemplations, thus providing me with immeasurable perspective. Many thanks for their insights written in engaging words. Without them this book would not exist.

My mother, Anne Imperi, who showed endless enthusiasm for my project and always asked, "So, how's the book coming?" She brought excitement to the project and treasured the copies of individual reflections I shared with her for advice, tucking them into a special file and showing them to visitors. It brings extraordinary joy to know that my mother is my greatest fan. As a guest writer, she contributed a reflection of her own, "Thoughts On a Day in May," the literary level of which I hope to achieve one day.

Evelyn Cado-Curtiss — the first person who gave affirmation to my writings and printed some of my reflections in booklet form more than a decade ago.

Gratitude and Appreciation

Editors extraordinaire:

Michelle Buckman — for her professional direction, insight, and skilled guidance, not to mention expert editing and transformation of my manuscript into an inspirational prayer journal. She shaped and molded what I had made a lame attempt to create, thus guiding me to the book within the manuscript. Also, for her encouragement and belief in my writing, and adding some poetic style along the way.

Kathy W. Larkin — a masterful wordsmith who constantly offered encouragement, support, and inspiration, throughout her endless editing and re-editing and who gave this book — and me — her heart, her pencil, and so many of her hours. She shared her expertise gently, and was always willing to help me even amidst her busy family life.

Virginia Carnahan — who help in the early stages with her charming phrases and shapes.

Without these three talented ladies, this book would not exist in its current state of excellence.

My encouragers: Those who read a few reflections in the early stages and praised them —"Stunning!"— offered words of encouragement —"So excited about your book!"— or prodded me —"Can't wait to see your first edition!" Lisa Ota, Susan Weaver, Chris Mishoe, Emmett Smith, Amy Bartos, Anne Todt, Beth Milwid, Melinda Slagle, Kogie Moodley, and Janice Loebbaka, Mary Sue Dempsey, Mary Karabinos. And other wonderful well-wishers who offered Congratulations! were excited and promised to become a reader, or just asked "How's the book coming?": Karen Mastriani, Jesse Smith, Karen and Jenna Woo, Sherran Blair, Amy Sugar-Carter, Margaret Wolf, Dr. Richard K. Fitzgerald, Tony and Marsha Pesa, Deb Newman, Marie Adamo, Cheryl Wheeler, John David Short, Sherry Bartley, Elizabeth Michalski, Gianna Vennari, Brian and Beth Mishoe, Lapointee Bryant, Rebecca Wenell, Brandon, Morgan, and Noah. And so, I kept writing.

Beloved, thoughtful and attentive souls — who sent cards, emails, letters, gifts; talked on the phone, met me for coffee, offered ideas, and kept me company along the way to encourage me to stay the course —willing to do whatever I needed.

The Sisters at the Convent of Saint Birgitta, who welcomed me into their lovely and serene chapel whenever I needed an intimate connection with the Eucharistic Presence of Jesus. Many insights were revealed to me there.

Individual gratitudes:

Debra Englander — an accomplished professional in the publishing world; a coach of extraordinary talent and experience; a friendly advisor with an engaging voice and affable personality — always attentive and poised. It was my privilege to work with her.

Doug Bean — for offering enthusiasm, supporting me through *The Catholic Times*, publishing articles, and endorsing my book.

L. Smith — a most astute, creative, introspective, and humble adviser.

Christy Day — a designer of intuitive talent who enhanced my words on the page through her unique approach to design and layout; and for her endless patience with this author.

Denise H. and Julie F. — sweet and caring, not only true friends, but always there with a kind word or thought, a quote for the book or marketing idea, an inspiration; always on the look-out for helpful items and ideas.

Maura — for convincing me it was enough, and for letting me know it was her favorite.

Kathy and Lucian — for their words and phrases that were better than mine; for their willingness and honest advice; for hours of assistance — I was never alone.

Serena Smith — for her photos, her technical prowess, and for encouraging me without knowing.

Suzanne Smith — who has a unique perspective and always knows the final answer, whenever I ask. Her keen eye and attention to detail are remarkable.

And most especially to Bradley Communications — Steve and Bill Harrison — who started it all with their Get Published Now Program. My first coach, Raia King, who gently guided me in the beginning. Debra Englander, who had all the answers and gave them to me, multiple times; held my hand when I needed it; and accompanied me to the end of the rainbow. Many advisors and authors who helped me in various ways throughout the process. Individually and collectively, they taught me how to write, how to market, and how to publish, and in the process became friends. Some of their names are Geoffrey Berwind, Cristina Smith, Sarah Brown, Mary Lou Reid, Trish Roberts, Suzette Webb, Stanley Robertson, Claire Doney, Joe McCallister, and others who have come and gone. You championed my efforts at every step, and kept me motivated with the inspiring ideas and practical tips I needed to create a book I've been blessed to write, and of which I am proud.

Quotes and Resources

INTRODUCTION

1. George Washington Carver. AZQuotes.com, Wind and Fly LTD,2022. https://www.azquotes.com/quote/50328, accessed March 30, 2022.
2. St. Teresa of Calcutta. AZQuotes.com, Wind and Fly LTD, 2022.
3. https://www.azquotes.com/quote/292124, accessed February 01, 2022.
4. Thomas Merton. AZQuotes.com, Wind and Fly LTD, 2022. https://www.azquotes.com/quote/857015, accessed February 01, 2022.

PART I

CHAPTER I

1. Chris Hazell. "Nature and the Soul," Chris Hazell.com, /?s=nature-and-the-soul, accessed February 01, 2022.
2. St. Teresa of Avila. Aleteia.org. https://aleteia.org/2017/04/24/the-tree-that-is-beside-the-running-water-is-fresher-and-gives-more-fruit/, accessed February 9, 2022.
3. St. Teresa of Calcutta. AZQuotes.com, Wind and Fly LTD, 2022. https://www.azquotes.com/quote/376339, accessed February 01, 2022.
4. Christine Valters Paintner, *Earth Our Original Monastery* (Notre Dame, IN: Sorin Books, 2020), xv.

CHAPTER II

1. Pope Francis, *The Church of Mercy* (Chicago, Illinois: Loyola Press, 2014), 11.
2. Becca Stevens, *Love Heals* (Nashville, TN: Thomas Nelson, 2017), 22.
3. St. Teresa of Avila. AZQuotes.com, Wind and Fly LTD, 2022. https://www.azquotes.com/quote/13544, accessed February 01, 2022.
4. Quoted in Blaise Arminjon, S.J., *The Cantata of Love* (San Francisco, CA: Ignatius Press, 1988), 18.

PART II — SPRING

1. Therese of Lisieux. AZQuotes.com, Wind and Fly LTD, 2022. https://www.azquotes.com/quote/364507, accessed February 01, 2022.
2. Arminjon, S.J., *Cantata*, 174.
3. Francis de Sales, *An Introduction to the Devout Life* (Charlotte, NC: Tan Books, 2010). https://wellbeing.gmu.edu/famous-quotes-on-prayer-and-well-being/, accessed February 01, 2022.
4. Charles Dickens Quotes. BrainyQuote.com, BrainyMedia Inc, 2022. https://www.brainyquote.com/quotes/charles_dickens_393445, accessed January 26, 2022.
5. St. Irenaeus. https://swordinariate.blogspot.com/2015/03/the-knot-of-eves-disobedience-was.html
6. Ignatian Spirituality. https://www.ignatianspirituality.com/teach-me-to-be-generous/, accessed February 02, 2022.

7. Gordon B. Hinckley. AZQuotes.com, Wind and Fly LTD, 2022. https://www.azquotes.com/quote/132865, accessed January 27, 2022.
8. Arminjon, S.J., *Cantata,* 283.
9. Mother Angelica, Foundress of EWTN, Eternal Word Television Network.
10. Arminjon, S.J., *Cantata,* 281.
11. St. Thomas Aquinas. (20+) TAN Academy—Posts | Facebook. https://www.facebook.com/TanAcademyHomeschool/posts/god-is-an-artist-and-the-universe-is-his-work-of-art-st-thomas-aquinasthe-founda/2958745857680194/, accessed January 26, 2022.

PART II — SUMMER

1. Pope Francis, "Gospel Calls Us to Trusting Abandonment to God," August, 9, 2020, Angelus Address. VaticanNews.va https://www.vaticannews.va/en/pope/news/2020-08/gospel-calls-us-to-abandon-ourselves-to-god-with-trust.html, accessed February 4, 2022.
2. St. Therese of Lisieux. LittleFlower.org. https://www.littleflower.org/prayers/pearls-of-wisdom/st-thereses-wisdom-prayer/.
3. Lisieux.https://www.LittleFlower.org./st-therese-daily-devotional/perfumes-of-jesus/, accessed February 12, 2022.
4. St. Teresa of Calcutta. Quotespedia.org. https://www.quotespedia.org/authors/m/mother-teresa/yesterday-is-gone-tomorrow-has-not-yet-come-we-have-only-today-let-us-begin-mother-teresa/, accessed February 4, 2022.
5. Crowfoot Blackfoot. JeffreySward.com. https://www.jeffreysward.com/editorials/quote.htm, accessed February 9, 2022.
6. Vatican Archives, NAB. https://www.vatican.va/archiveENG0839/_PLG.HTM, accessed February 7, 2022.
7. Lisieux.https://www.littleflower.org/st-therese-daily-devotional/our-hearts-were-made-for/, accessed February 4, 2022.

PART II — AUTUMN

1. Ralph Waldo Emerson Quotes. BrainyQuote.com, BrainyMedia Inc, 2022. https://www.brainyquote.com/quotes/ralph_waldo_emerson_125813, accessed January 26, 2022.
2. Ralph Waldo Emerson. RFQK.com. rfqk.com/natures-secret.html.
3. William Shakespeare, *Romeo and Juliet.* https://holidappy.com/quotes/roses-quotes. Accessed February 3, 2022.
4. Matthew Kelly, *Mustard Seeds* (Cincinnati, OH: Beacon Publishing, 1998), 16.
5. Cecile Smith, *Connecting with God in the Garden* (Columbus, OH: Montorio Societa, 2022), 14,15, 72.
6. Aesop.HarbinHollow.com.https://harbinhollow.com/blogs/news/gratitude-turns-what-we-have-into-enough-aesop, accessed February 9, 2022.
7. Albert Einstein Quotes. BrainyQuote.com, BrainyMedia Inc, 2022. https://www.brainyquote.com/quotes/albert_einstein_136891, accessed January 26, 2022.

PART II — WINTER

1. John Steinbeck. GoodReads.com. https://www.goodreads.com/quotes/54619-what-good-is-the-warmth-of-summer-without-the-cold, accessed February 5, 2022.
2. St. Clement. Catholic365.com. https://www.catholic365.com/article/12681/sunsets-to-sunrise.html, accessed February 9, 2022.
3. Dale Carnegie. AZQuotes.com, Wind and Fly LTD, 2022. https://www.azquotes.com/quote/536361, accessed January 27, 2022.
4. St. Teresa of Calcutta, "I thirst" — a letter from Mother Teresa to her sisters. CatholicLifeMinistries.org. www.catholiclifeministries.org/2019/04/18/4228/, accessed February 9, 2022.
5. St. Margaret Mary Alacoque, Words of Jesus to St. Margaret Mary Alacoque. TheRealPresence.org. www.therealpresence.org/eucharst/tes/quotes2.html, accessed February 9, 2022.
6. St. Boniface. "A letter on the martyrdom of St. Boniface" quoted in the Liturgy of the Hours. Aleteia.org. https://aleteia.org/daily-prayer/monday-june-5/, accessed February 9, 2022.

About the Author

Cecile Smith is a lover of nature, casual gardener, author, singer, movement specialist, former homeschool mother, and friend. She enjoys spending time outdoors — her favorite place to contemplate, sip coffee, walk, and talk with God.

She lives and works in central Ohio, where her life is filled with family and friends! Her grown children, growing grandchildren, her century-old Mother, and siblings are scattered across the country. She also enjoys many precious friends who provide sweet companionship — and is grateful for all these blessings.

Cecile writes from her garden — immersed in Nature — where she is always in pursuit of God's presence here on Earth. She thrives in sunshine and sits or stands in the morning sun no matter the weather. Likewise, she endeavors to always watch the sun set.

A contributor to *The Catholic Times* Newspaper of Columbus, Ohio, *Connecting with God in the Garden* is her first book.

Cecile shares thought-provoking reflections and welcomes comments from her readers through her website at www.CecileSmith.com.

CPSIA information can be obtained
at www.ICGtesting.com
Printed in the USA
LVHW060346130922
728229LV00026B/520